MEDIUMS

Vol. 1

CONTEXTS

# Pratt Sessions

# Mediums

# David Erdman
# New Architectural Mediums

In Pratt Sessions, half of our talks will introduce the subject of New Architectural Mediums. We are intentionally conflating medium and media. The purpose of such a focus is to intensify a number of standing debates and to stimulate nerve endings within the discipline and profession that we (at the GAUD) feel are important and will remain important in the coming decades. In short, it is an effort to unleash the limits of the (now) somewhat traditional software-based representational media that enable architectural drawing, modeling, and prototyping as well as unleash the temporal processes (mediums) found in buildings (artificial/natural light, horticulture, screens and graphics, among others) as a means to investigate their potentials from an explicitly post-digital, post-geometrical vantage point. We aim to examine the extent to which we could understand them as highly synthetic, design-driven components of our architectural and urban environments, and to move them into the realm of live experience. Each of the Pratt Sessions participants offers a vantage point on the subjects of architectural media/mediums, and each pairing raises specific questions surrounding the prospect of those subjects: namely what is an "architectural" media and/or medium and why would either be valuable now or in the future?

From signaling and patterning (both modes of communication-based media) to a broadening of our understanding of the perceptual modes of architecture through the prostheses of various live media, to an examination of the differences and similarities of graphically and cinematically induced architecture, the three Pratt Sessions collected here definitively trace an emerging and important discourse. Supported by invigorated track records of built work and/or writing to underpin their claims and the points being made by our coveted participants, the discussions and presentations encapsulated here present concise snippets, glimpses of how our understanding of media might change as a discipline and profession. It is equally important to note that each practice, participant, designer, and thinker operates within a multitude of media and mediums, bringing them together primarily through the contemporary experience of the human subject in relation to the architectural environments they study or design. Finally, it is worth noting that each speaker diminishes the idea that there is any such thing as singular "essential" architectural media or medium (as has been historically espoused via innumerable architectural treatises on space, light, movement), while also implicitly insisting upon the idea that one would only arrive at a particular experience, or at a specific configuration/combination of media through architectural design.

The framing for the discussions is meant to be provocative, theoretical, and historical. The association of architecture and media may seem odd. Media is ephemeral; that which is not permanent, it's fleeting. Mediums are equally intangible, slippery. Whether one considers pop cultural media, branding, graphics, signage, or mediums like light, air, or water, none would be associated with the conventional cultural assumptions about architecture, its permanence, its object orientation, or its weight. Media and mediums are the stuff architecture contains as opposed to the "skin and bones" of Architecture proper with a capital "A." Importantly, these disassociations between architecture, media, and mediums further reinforce contemporary and historical propensities toward architectures of purity, autonomy, and away from everything capital and commercial for which the fluidity and expendable qualities of media stand. In short, the following sessions examine, perturb, and irritate the idea that media and mediums are the things that one might consider "outside" of architecture and opportunistically include them as a necessary tool kit for architects, our entrepreneurial thinking, our innovation, and the expansion of our practice and discourse.

These three sessions also recognize that both media and mediums have always been enmeshed in architecture; though perhaps simply not historicized or canonized as such, which might be another way of saying architecture has an ephemeral, superficial, and fleeting yet parallel counterpart. Drawing upon quantum theory, one could understand this parallelism as the simultaneous co-existing and enmeshing of alternative realities through architecture and its live experiences; more specifically through its potential and perceived dimensionalities. Underscoring this are two projects which are perhaps radically misunderstood and/or under explored for their potential; the

Pantheon and the Parthenon. Each separately introduces medium and media as necessary parts of architecture: the Pantheon—a building designed around a medium, one window shaping light—and the Parthenon—a vessel-container for many narrative and pop cultural stories (communicative media), including its war story frieze and caryatids etched, sculpted, and painted into the building.

An important commonality among these two examples touches upon their illusive aspects and the fact that they tinker with dimensionality. Elements—architectural and otherwise—shift between 2D, 3D, and 4D. There is an *entanglement* of media; here again borrowing from the lexicon of quantum theory and the notion of "entangled" electrons that form parallel universes. In each of these projects architecture, sculpture, drawing, graphics, painting, air, and light vibrate in and out of focus, shift scales, alter perceived depths and densities of content or information, allowing one to experience a rich texture of spaces, simultaneously evoking what today might be called an "intermedia" experience. These surprisingly antiquated and quintessential architectural projects also introduce how buildings can convert specific media "technologies" and mediums (often from other disciplines, other professions or literally from "outside") and galvanize them into live architectural experiences. They embrace contamination and use other media and mediums as fodder, making them a reciprocal and inextricable agent in the architecture; they are not "contained" but activated and activating the subjects immersed within them.

While the history of this is fascinating, ripe for exploration and implicit in these sessions, a subject of greater interest at the GAUD is the value of understanding the use of media and mediums at the turn of the twenty-first century—is it valuable or not? From the digital to the post-digital, the Pratt Sessions speculate that it may be worth extending our understanding of media beyond the representational and the generative; beyond modeling, drawing, prototyping software and to engage in alternative emerging forms of live communication. This opens the door to explore the intersection of where the representational becomes experiential or conceived in real-time. Each of the participants as individuals and in their pairs is curated to create hinge points of this discourse—expanding it and reinscribing both its futures and its histories.

Circling back to the above noted point and in a broader context, it is perfectly reasonable to wonder why this examination of media and mediums might be important to a graduate school of architecture today or for the future of its students. In short, we hope to demystify the many media and mediums available to students—from software and robots to green walls and energy production—and give them a framework for understanding how to engage them as architects and within the realm of their design work. This strain of the Pratt Sessions thus lauds new concepts of architectural media. It sees this discourse and debate as necessary for a contemporary graduate student's education and sees the subject as bona fide theoretical, conceptual, and design substance key to their education and the profession into which they will enter; and hopefully alter. These first three Pratt Sessions on Architectural Media and Mediums act humbly as the starting point. They are a foundation that welcomes a broader understanding of these concepts with the hope that they will offer our students and the GAUD community an opportunity to use technology in deep and meaningful ways that enable them to engage extra-disciplinary audiences and expand architecture thinking, its role in leadership and its potential praxes.

# Eric Höweler

# Marcelo
# Spina

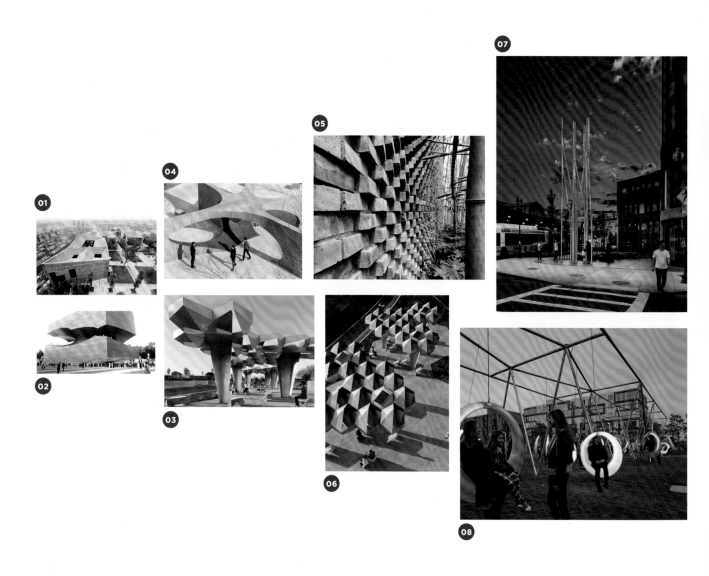

# Introduction

## DAVID ERDMAN

It is my pleasure to introduce our two guests this evening, Eric Höweler and Marcelo Spina, who will explore the theme of New Architectural Mediums. They have both struggled with and negotiated this topic with skill and tireless ambition in their teaching and practice. Trained to **draw by hand**, educated at the **peak of the digital turn**, and practicing in the **post-digital/post-human era**, their work builds upon this significant shift; one which sees our world and our subjectivity as increasingly mediated.

Eric and Marcelo, with their counterparts Meejin Yoon and Georgina Huljich, are deeply committed practitioners and academics. They are among the few who have launched their practices through academia, write about their work actively, and who have graduated into a substantial portfolio of work that spans the gamut from exhibitions and prototypes; includes small, medium, and large buildings of many types; bridges a spectrum of public and private work; contains an impressive amount of completed work; and reflects **unwavering commitment to speculation**.

Representational media are only an undercurrent supporting a deeper project. It is the experience of the "*subject*," their **reception and perception** of the work, and finally how one interacts with the work that shapes their design ingenuity and galvanizes their proprietary methods. To this extent, the issue of **live experience**, how it is mediated, and how each firm deploys a multitude of media are central to this evening's discussion. Instead of seeking common ground between our two guests (which may be obvious for some in the audience), first it is perhaps useful to examine their differences.

Höweler + Yoon's work has a **stereotomic quality**. **01** **02** It is often **chamfered, sliced, and booleaned** **03** as if eroding a larger solid. **04** Figural voids permeate the work and imbue it with a sense of **porosity and buoyancy**. Equally present are vibrant textural arrays **05** that orient and give direction to **open-ended fields and aggregates**. **06** Combined, this consortium of methods, materials, and form instigates a series of two-dimensional and four-dimensional effects. **Compressive and expansive sensations** in concert with **lush yet subtle haptic interferences** that wash over you, in what they might refer to as a "**silent noise**" is unescapable. However, one of the most distinguishing characteristics of their work is the concerted effort to mix media or an **intermedia approach**. **07**

Sensors, lights, actuators, and screens are enmeshed into many of their projects, **08** giving them a space and depth that expands into the **virtual realm**. The medium of space is often intensely collapsed or expanded, where the "reach" of the work might well exceed its physical footprint or even the necessity to be at the site. Media is a means of being at once very specific and local and at the same time urban and far reaching. It is used to a space between "signal and noise," to use their words.

P-A-T-T-E-R-N-S' work, on the other hand, has a **delicacy and superficial quality** that imbues it with an uncanny degree of combined **ephemerality and objecthood**. **09** Lines, textures, and patterns are neither ornament nor simply derivations of the geometries from which they are born. **10** Instead, they are somewhat autonomous, **11** **resisting and/or contradicting the surfaces** into which they are embedded. I see this as a way of making lines, patterns, and textures **active, material**, and **experiential**. They are not representational, **12** but **full-scale networks** one moves through and in which one, surprisingly, finds them not necessarily aligned with the massing or enclosure. To this degree, they are able to conjure an additional **experiential dimension**, **13** where these patterns levitate off the object as much as they are tethered to it. It is a productive tension. Artificial lighting, color, shade, and shadow intensify the actuation of these various graphic moves, **14** giving them a **virtual, elusive depth and coarseness**. In this way one feels different parts of the sensorium and different types of media wafting in and out of focus when engaging their work. **15**

While both designers galvanize a wide spectrum of representational and construction technologies, what is perhaps most important in the context of the Pratt Sessions is the degree of **saturation and immersion** present in their work; by entirely different means. Both engage the **artifice of multiple media**, but one starts with the solid (Höweler + Yoon) and the other with the surface (P-A-T-T-E-R-N-S). They harness and shape media in different ways, yet the **layers of dimensionality and the textures of experience** are present in both of their work. The projects are so mediated that is difficult to understand these designs from a traditional parti, from an illustration or from a single perspective. One could go as far as to say that, while they have a **high degree of objecthood**, they do not have a clear outside. They oscillate within and **contaminate their contexts** while dynamically **shape-shifting** before your eyes and under your feet. In this way, they are using media in new ways, ones that engage our subjectivity, our relationships to our surroundings, and how we understand the simultaneous **reality and virtuality of architecture**; making them exemplars par excellence for the inaugural Pratt Session on this subject.

# Eric Höweler

**BOSTON, MA**

We've been talking about signal-to-noise because we are suggesting that architecture is a broadcast medium. It has always been a broadcast medium, but how can we think about it in contemporary terms?

The example I use is the Gothic cathedral as a special effects machine. The cathedral enlisted structure, glass, light, sound, and smell to create an immersive environment that was meant to communicate through narrative and sheer awe and wonder; it was an architecture of persuasion.

With modernism we saw a different kind of architecture. An architecture that was still broadcasting and communicating, but the signal was different. It was about the skyscraper as a signal of stability or success with a commercial brand at the top. We talk about lighting shifting from illumination to communication. Before, we used light to render form sculptural, and now we use light to broadcast or celebrate a festivity. We think architecture has the capacity to serve as broadcast medium, to augment communication signals. Our sense is that a contemporary engagement with the public realm is always heavily mediated by

our devices and how we might think about public space through these devices.

We've been working in different modes, thinking about the material and media as the substance of architecture. However, a lot of the projects deal with the public realm. How is that encounter in the public realm historically about the kind of informal or the unexpected? How do we see the public realm today as a means to enact a political project?

We did a project in Boston for a new government building—we call it Signal Spire. We thought, "How could we design a structure within the city that communicates in the way that the church spire and the church bells do? How do we create a kind of signaling device, a landmark in the city, in a contemporary way?"

We took the idea of the bundle or bundling tubes together to represent the different neighborhoods within Boston. If a signal can be decoded, it's somehow communicating. Within Boston there's a building that is a signal spire and there's a rhyme that goes with it. If you're from Boston and you know the rhyme you can decode the signal. You always know if it's a "steady blue" then tomorrow will be a sunny day.

Thinking about signals within Boston, how do we take a new kind of signal to create a broadcast structure in the city? The city also has a 311 system for urban problems like a pothole or a traffic light. We thought we could use that data set, because that's an incredibly rich, geo-tagged data set that is very finely organized. However, with media structures, it's important to ask, "What's the content and who's going to make the content?" This is an open source data set that the City of Boston is constantly updating. We grabbed that data set, we filtered it, and we broadcast it back into the piece. The piece is a structure, but it's also the programming that filters out the content.

Another project we did was the Dubai Expo pavilion. We were invited with Tod Machover from the MIT Media Lab to develop a pavilion around the topic of empathy. The question was, can we create a place whereby people would be trained to be empathic? Empathy is not simply innate, it can be engineered. And so, with Tod Machover, who is a composer, the idea was to create a space where you would experience a series of highly composed experiences, and you would emerge somehow transformed and empathic. Tod developed the performances on the interior, and we developed the structure that would house them. The structure consisted of a series of chambers of increasing size that you would experience as you climbed up, and then the cascading carved out space was the descent as you emerged from the empathy pavilion.

A new project that we're working on is a proposal for the Schuylkill River in Philadelphia. As a city between two rivers,

Höweler + Yoon, Crisscross Signal Spire, Boston, MA, 2014

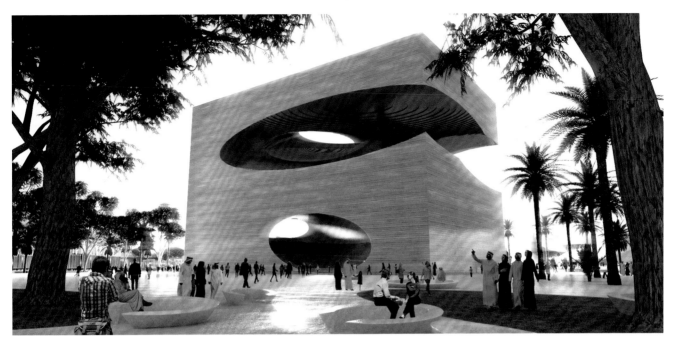

Höweler + Yoon, Empathy Pavilion, Dubai Expo 2020, Dubai, UAE, 2016

Philadelphia emerged through industry and transportation. Our proposal intends to bring people back to that river front to engage with the ecologies of an urban nature. It's an outdoor classroom where you can immerse yourself in the river. It brings you down to the water level so you can experience the river from a new vantage point. The technology is quite simple. You have to flood the ballast of this submarine to get it to control capsize in such a way that creates that vantage point. To prove this, we built a prototype and deployed it in the river. Verifying the chambers, we developed a leak, but at the end of the day we managed to stabilize it in a condition that would demonstrate the capacity to immerse you in the river so that you could experience the transformed river ecology of the Philadelphia waterways.

One last project I wanted to present is a memorial to the MIT police officer that was killed by the Boston Marathon bombers. MIT's motto is *Mens et Manus*, Hand and Mind, to which they added *Fortis*. We thought, what is strength? The proposal was to create a figure that would create a conspicuous absence of a figure. We booleaned out a figure from this five-fingered form. We proposed to make it out of massive blocks of granite that would form an arch. As a contemporary building structure, that was somehow quite radical.

MIT funded it because it seemed to embody something about coming together, transferring loads, and achieving equilibrium through the balancing of those forces. We worked with John Ochsendorf, who is a historian and a structural engineer. He's been researching Inca masonry techniques for nesting and transferring loads. We worked with several engineers to develop a structural logic. It's basically all compression. There's no tension because all the forces are simply transferring from block to block. The geometry is such that the arch is so shallow that the thrust lines are almost horizontal as they start moving through the blocks.

We procured the stone blocks in Virginia and oversaw the fabrication, which was an incredible challenge. How do you take a block of stone that's 8 feet by 8 feet by 12 feet and carve it for two weeks with a robotic arm? In addition, the saw is wearing at a different rate than the stone. How do you achieve precision with a medium that is wearing in parallel? Every time the saw cuts, it needs to recalibrate.

The memorial is made up of thirty-three blocks of stone, erected over a winter with record snowfall in Boston. How do you see force? How do you know that the keystone is transferring loads to the ring stones and to the buttresses? You don't.

If you go to MIT's campus today, you'll see the memorial. It is for the police officer, but it is part of the everyday life—students move through it. They requested a boulder so we gave them the absence of that boulder.

*Eric Höweler and Marcelo Spina*

Höweler + Yoon, Collier Memorial, Cambridge, MA, 2014

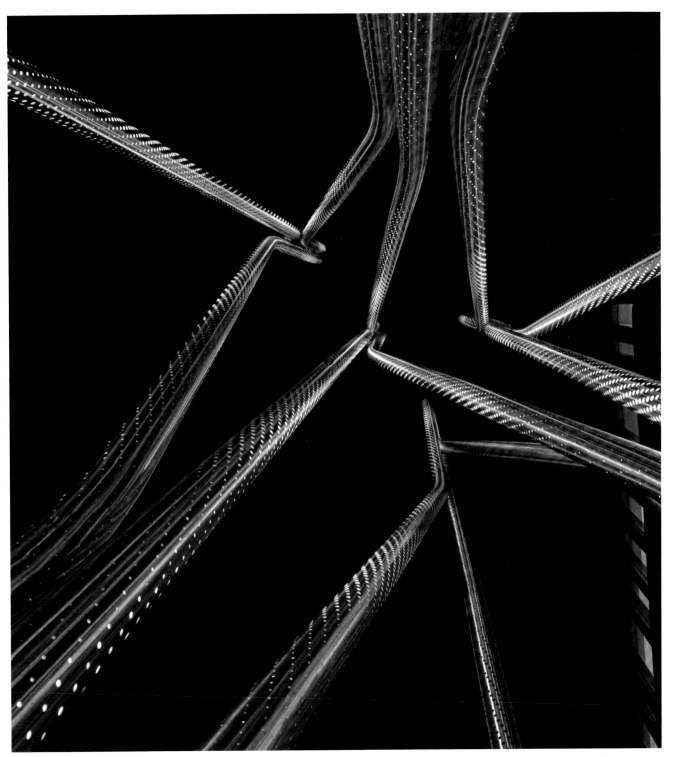

Höweler + Yoon, Crisscross Signal Spire, Boston, MA, 2014

Eric Höweler and Marcelo Spina

Höweler + Yoon, Swing Time, Boston, MA, 2014

Höweler + Yoon with Parallel Development, Aviary, Dubai, UAE, 2013

# Marcelo Spina

**LOS ANGELES, CA**

I'd like to approach the topic of new architectural mediums in terms of how one moves from ideas of medium as a means, to mediums as agency. The problems that we have today are very different than those we dealt with twenty years ago. Of course, there is the environmental problem and as a result, what we define as an ethical approach to this problem; how we position alternatives to mainstream ideas of sustainability. The problems of finance and economy as one of architecture's driving forces. And then culture, and our reaction and interest with problems of estrangement. We're very interested in the problem of cross-over between subject and context. All of this relates to the problem of the relevance or irrelevance of the icon. Our commitment isn't to renounce the problem of the icon, but to suggest that there may be alternative ways we can work with this issue.

At any given time in our office, things take the form of drawings. We're committed to a certain degree of autonomy in what we do.

As in, building for building's sake, and project for project's sake. These things can exist separate from the world of architecture and from the "real."

We're also committed to putting these things out there, even if they are only images. Conveying a certain kind of sensate aspect, a form of engagement, even by mystery, somehow could imply that the architectural object at some point completely withdraws.

Over a summer a few years ago, we did a competition entry for four museums in Budapest. We assembled the techniques of glitching, which was connected to a graphic idea that then was projected back into the form to make it indecipherable, and more ambiguous or indeterminate. What it took was to basically put architecture in context, in a very different context, and isolate or associate itself with context. Also, to somehow potentially change context.

When I talk about icons I talk about something that is ultimately a reception of architecture. We don't make icons, we make buildings or projects. Culture makes icons, people and their assumptions make icons, and this is an interesting project to portray these ideas.

Of all the recent competitions, the League of Shadows Graduation Pavilion at SCI-Arc was a competition we really didn't want to win. We wanted to do a smart job and lose. There was one simple brief to this project, it needed to hold up to 1,300 people in a shadow on an early September day for a big graduation that goes on in a parking lot just beside SCI-Arc.

In looking at the SCI-Arc campus, we thought, we'll just put this thing in the corner of the 4th Street Bridge, which is a very transitive location. Our second thought was that if you're going to place a big pavilion on the ground, it will become stagnant. It is going to take up a lot of parking spaces but if you build upward, it will diminish the footprint on the ground. The third thing, which was potentially the most important, was that if you calculate the shadows—and we just got lucky—you could cast enough shadow to create a band shell. Something that exists as an object, does what it needs to do, and then recedes as an

P-A-T-T-E-R-N-S, New National Gallery and Ludwig Museum [NNGA & LMU], Budapest, Hungary 2014

P-A-T-T-E-R-N-S with SOM Los Angeles, Olympia, Los Angeles, CA, 2022

institutional beacon in the corner.

The paradox between the muteness and iconicity of this project relies on the fact that it has a clear outline. That dichotomy was quite important to us. The fact that you could have architecture with this two-sidedness was significant, and it's something we're very much interested in these days.

After fifteen years of living in Los Angeles, you are forced to theorize what's really going on. Somehow, it's nice to be working in your city, especially when the city is dramatically changed by big forces of development and densification in the core district.

Our Olympia project sits to the left of a big tower—a Ritz-Carlton hotel, which is one of the widest towers in downtown. Our tower is relatively skinny in size, sitting right on the freeway. This project is a collaboration with SOM Los Angeles, and is for a Hong Kong-based developer. The project called for a vertical neighborhood. What was significant here was determining how you might bring some of the more discursive ideas found in smaller work to a project of this size. In a way, we had to work with the void as much as with the solids.

Ideas connecting private space with community space up in the air were part of the discussion right from the start. Of course, these ideas addressed connecting three buildings that will be completed in different phases. It couldn't connect them physically, but connect them visually so they become individual parts of a singular project. Ultimately, closing with that language on potential slabs demonstrates that this building, which is 95 percent residential with two hotels, would be revealed by the mere language that this thing is not completely smooth.

Two main issues arose as the project developed materially. One involved developing the voids. The voids are capitalized with the soffits of the areas that basically hold the amenities. The other is that the building is made entirely out of glass to manage environmental and heat gains so you have a bit of a self-shading, but only through two kinds of glass.

At different times of day, you have something that is a little bit more transparent, and hopefully in the evening one could begin to read the striation diagonally across the three towers. Further, going into more detail, across the towers the same system is used to maximize the economy and yet produce disruptions. As this disruption of the slabs happens in midair, we looked at the importance of how to deny or mute 90 percent of the building—this is not something that developers would be too eager for—or how you might make a grand gesture of overlapping slabs where you have two levels of amenities and special floors where people can be closer to communal activity; to create not only a canvas for architectural innovation, or spectacle, but also a canvas for artists or collaborators to project media or to reconceive of that. Especially as you begin to see the towers, the three of them together begin to weave through the spaces when the towers are apart, or when you approach them and the towers start to appear too close to each other.

P-A-T-T-E-R-N-S, League of Shadows, Los Angeles, CA, 2013

P-A-T-T-E-R-N-S with Maxi Spina Architects, Jujuy Redux, Rosario, Argentina, 2012

P-A-T-T-E-R-N-S with Maxi Spina Architects, Jujuy Redux, Rosario, Argentina, 2012

P-A-T-T-E-R-N-S, Victory Healthcare, North Hollywood, CA, 2018

Eric Höweler and Marcelo Spina

# Conversation

## ERIC HÖWELER AND MARCELO SPINA

**David Erdman (DE):** Eric, you brought up a provocative point about illumination turning into communication and the idea of architecture as a broadcast medium. That's great language for some of the things that are latent in a lot of struggles of how we're designing and how these media might begin to interact with an architectural environment or audience. The problem of content is a classic problem, and in the Crisscross Signal Spire you dealt with this by "filtering" it. The data collection from the 311 system was an engine to produce the aesthetic of the pulsing light, which abstains you (as the author) from having to assign the content a Venturian description (here emphasizing the "sign" of "assign")—the signal is muted or muffled to some extent.

Marcelo, I was seeing a very different approach in your strategy for the museum competition entry, where the diachronic patterning is "noise" that is preventing us from being able to read the building in a normally geometrically conventional manner. Edges get feathered or the diagonals are disrupting the massing of the building. Is a building a communicator? How do we understand icons as something that is received or broadcast?

All of this still comes down to the problem of content. Both of you seem to be suggesting that you can mute it. You could never say the medium is the message, as Marshall McLuhan did, because the message is constantly being obscured or filtered. When the message is so lucid and legible, does it delaminate itself from the architecture to the extent that we can longer understand it as architecture?

**Eric Höweler (EH):** We are explicitly working with content. How do you produce enough of it? And then, what does it mean? We are trapped by the Venturian question. If you're broadcasting all this code, is someone decoding it? Is there a similar kind of poem that people will learn to read the architecture? However, I think it's still a type of provisional broadcast, testing the medium to see if it can be legible or if it simply produces an effect. I think what Marcelo is working on is how to take a superabundance of signals and produce material effects; producing graphic content that's architectural.

**DE:** It brings up the idea of legibility that I believe relates to distance. You referred to it as "reading." Something that I find so interesting in both of your work is the willful acceptance of immersion and obfuscation. As the live experience seems to be important in the work and as a result the subject can never get far enough away from it to read it; they are in it. Even at extreme distances you have both mastered techniques that allow you to exfoliate the local effects of the architecture from further away; it still feels immersive or has a "long reach."

**Marcelo Spina (MS):** I believe that if the building is not legible, what you're trying to do is not legible. It's really a problem in a way. What we're trying to do is somehow either delay legibility or complicate it. Not to the point where it becomes complete atrophy—I think that would be illegibility altogether—but to do so in a way where the legibility isn't as clear. Or, where the legibility you are getting is not representative of the real thing; where you can't count how many floors a building is, therefore you can't know how big it is. Or, a building looks bigger than what it truly is. For me, this is a simpler, mundane thing that has to do with the state of distraction through which one interacts with buildings.

**DE:** If the goal of a developer is to produce a unique experience, whether it's retail or housing, that gets you to stay there longer, to extend the duration, I think that is where the image doesn't succeed because you get it right away. You get it, and you split.

Whereas, a practice of *intermedia*—one that is more like the environment we browse on our phones or we all work through on our desk tops—is more akin to the collapses and expanses one senses in both of your work. Eric, with yours, the subject is literally required to shift from the phone, to lighting, to touch. There are weird layers of how one might engage that environment. If you were to talk with Apple, Google, or Samsung in terms of how they're designing their environments, that idea of *intermedia layering* and engagement, is precisely the idea that the environment can't be legible if you want an extended duration. You can't snap it back into a Venturian duck. Do you agree with that?

**MS:** I think that brings up an interesting issue. The problem with the Venturian duck was that you had a building below with an advertisement above—image and content or image and form were separated. Right now, you can effectively merge these ideas. Between the flickering and the differentiation of those two ideas, there exists a lot of possibility for attraction by irritation in our case, or attraction by interaction in Eric's case, that can take place. To which extent it's successful commercially, it's hard to say, but I think the point is to question how you can innovate new forms of content that will translate all the way into a typology, beyond a facade.

**DE:** I'm bringing it up because you said a client would want you to do something legible, and I'm questioning that. If you look at the logics behind contemporary retail environments and developers, they're centered on a multitude of experiences that can produce a longer delay. And so, whether it produces profit, I would accuse the discourse of abstaining from engaging with that contemporary temporal modality and economy; for the sake of sustaining an antiquated notion of critical autonomy and practice. But I would go further to suggest that there is a cultural aptitude involving habitation and duration that is looking for a much more multi-valent set of experiences and in which architecture discourse (and the profession) should participate and play a significant role.

**MS:** Depending on the audience, I think in some cases you can get your way. Particularly with the big project we're working on in downtown Los Angeles. You have an investment of more than a billion dollars and a massive view that will redefine the downtown for miles. So, everyone wants to know what's going to happen, and what's going to be seen when you approach downtown from the freeway. They don't want to repeat the ugly towers around, yet, they don't want it to cost more than the ugly towers. There must be a way to say, "This is what we're doing and this is what you're getting," at that scale. In a smaller approach, I don't think you can produce work as kind of a magic, or let's say, how an artist would do it. As in, they receive a commission and that's basically their content.

**DE:** You don't think that applies to the urban scale?

**MS:** At least not at that scale. It could apply to retail. They will do it slightly differently and would purposely remove the architect from that equation. Because, for example, the architect will have issues with how somebody might bastardize the proportions of a building or, the inclusion of signage. We want to say, "Well, let's get signage out there but let's have artists address that need." For example, you could project massive

P-A-T-T-E-R-N-S with SOM Los Angeles, Olympia, Los Angeles, CA, 2022

images but that's not the type of signage that generates revenue.

**EH:** You said you don't design icons, but in a way a client is asking you for an icon, "show me a new LA." I think you're producing a different kind of icon, one that's not stable; one that's constantly shimmering. How does that translate into a new kind of visibility? I think this idea of the glitch; your eye goes to the glitch precisely because it's not quite stable. If a skyscraper is a design silhouette, and you're creating a silhouette that isn't stable, I think that's more attractive. These are economies of attention and architecture operates in these economies. When doing it at different scales, I wouldn't say, "Why wouldn't you go for the commercial content and the retail environment?" This is the realm that architecture could participate in.

One of our early projects that I didn't show was a sign. Our client was redeveloping a building and he said, "Can you build me a sign?" And we said, "Well, how do we hijack that sign into a two-sided LED screen that you can actually broadcast a live feed into and as you walk by your image is broadcast back to you?" It might cause you to slow down. That sort of deceleration was part of their strategy for retail. Can we get people to slow down through interactivity? We were okay with helping to reconsider that public realm. It's public space, but with a private broadcast. But I think there was cultural content in addition to a commercial benefit. That's where we were interested in using the sign as a public space-making condition using all media at our disposal. There was a steel frame, there was glass, there were all the architectural components, but then, there was this LED net. There was a choreography; a real-time feed into that net which created a different kind of delay. This was of course at a small scale. Scaling up to a bigger project, I think it would be interesting to apply similar techniques to a larger scale development.

**Sanford Kwinter (SK):** I would like to, in a way, penetrate a bit into the mind of a generation. Assume that the architect still has a soul. On one hand, what we heard is that the architect is essentially putting his or her creativity at the service of retail and of the developer. On the other hand, of the media industrial complex. But let's say the architect actually has a mandate of their own. Who do you work for? What can the architect contribute besides finding clever ways to further embed the citizen in an existing neuro-capitalist logic where the intention, the behaviors, the reflexes, the mindset, the thought patterns of the citizen are becoming subsumed by the existing culture? Or can the architect do very clever things to hack the system?

**DE:** There's a theory out there that the contemporary urban subject is bombarded by so much media that the project of

David Erdman (left), Marcelo Spina (middle), and Eric Höweler in conversation at Pratt Sessions 02

architecture is to peel that back. It's about media deprivation. The delight of architecture, the medium of architecture, is about its ability to abstain from that stuff. That's the purity and autonomy of Louis Kahn kicking out the sign, the delight of all the tropes of Greenberg's striated mediums and modernity.

There's a way to deal with intermedia, things that are mediatric on several levels and that have high degrees of saturation and immersion, but also bewilderingly delightful. That has nothing to do with the client. That has to do with awareness, subjectivity and how you're producing experiences and environments that are engaging people to wake up to a new kind of sensorium that's mediated in part by their phone and the things that they work with. Yet, somehow, it's not fatiguing, it's pleasurable. When I see the popular attraction to these guys' projects there's clearly something going on there; be it online visits or in person. The "project" has a soul, for sure. The work has a kind of gravity to it, and yet they don't make arguments that other architects are making today. I think that's kind of a beginning point for that project. It's how you develop that trajectory, which to some extent is unpredictable. You can't say, "I'm going to guarantee that," but you're willing to take the risk to play in that zone and try to figure that out.

**SK:** I do want to say that I didn't miss the way you were leading them with some of the language in your original engagement. Using words like experience, and especially suggesting that there was enormous room for the invention of new experience, and new ways of engaging an environment, but that word never came back. I could certainly read their work along those lines but they didn't. They purposely didn't. Let's just say that when I look for hope, I found it in what you were proposing, but I didn't think they were looking for it.

**EH:** The frame that David set up about experience, media, and the public realm is something we're interested in. The public realm has been radically transformed by technology. How does architecture participate in that? Could architecture create

attention, or create a pause within that sort of bombardment? To compete for attention in the media saturated environment is an arms race, it cannot be won. It can compete, say in Times Square, with absolute silence or masking.

We are committed to using architecture to create that enhanced sort of public realm in a capitalist urban context. How do you do that at the scale of a tall building? And how do you maintain that kind of project when you're in the service of a developer who is seeking differentiation? Often, people will come to us and say, "Your projects look high-tech. We want that image; can you provide that for us?" At that point, you're enlisted to create a high-tech image. But I think the idea that you can resist the collapse into an image by evolving interactivity is something that introduces the potential for resistance even while you're being enlisted to produce these icons. The risk is to not engage. That would be a generational position. Rather than say, "We don't like that developer stuff," we say, "Let's engage the developer, let's lend our thinking and our tools to that and see where we can find pockets of potential within that realm."

**MS:** Our interest specifically relies on building a kind of tension or dichotomy, that maybe continues a certain history of dialectics in architecture. We're interested in creating enough friction within the architectural object that it will simultaneously produce both autonomy and engagement. David spoke eloquently about experience, but I'm uncomfortable talking about experience in those terms. Not because it's untrue, but I would be worried to be too complicit when it comes to ideas of experience. The soul of the architect can be found in the idea of the calibration of more than one thing. It's not parametric, it's not a cohesive model that could be found in any given way of understanding one single model. It goes beyond that into understanding that within the friction, there is a kind of cascading of dichotomy. You could find buildings, or architecture, that are much more in tune with the images I was showing early on. They're not only a reaction and symptomatic to the context. Context matters, but in a certain way they push back on that context because it's not the same context as before. Technology and media are all around us, but architecture can, and has in my opinion, to do something with a degree of autonomy of building, and the history of building and the history of drawing buildings, and the history of media supporting and being projected or embedded within that. We do a lot to show or hide that tension so you don't have a clear A to B condition but you have a far more complex relationship between the state of beings.

**SK:** I'm glad I asked the question, because you gave a brilliant answer.

P-A-T-T-E-R-N-S, Budapest Museum of Ethnography, Budapest, Hungary, 2014

Höweler + Yoon, LoRezHiFi, Washington, DC, 2005

Höweler + Yoon, Light Drift - Intersect, Philadelphia, PA, 2010

Eric Höweler and Marcelo Spina

ZONE

# Sanford Kwinter

ZONE will ... th...
...inary perspective and through a
...mats. ZONE will publish essays on
...ture, econom... ...y and ...ba...
...ce and will inc... ...ograp...
...d technical d...iers, d...l of ...
...responses to formal questionnaires.

ZONE 1|2

...aural double issue examines the
...tical and perceptual transformations
...rrently redefining the contemporary

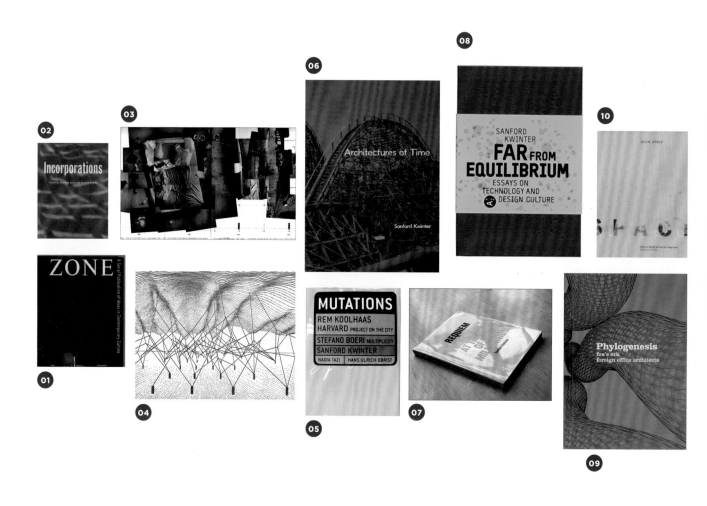

# Introduction

## DAVID ERDMAN

It's my pleasure to introduce our two speakers this evening, Sanford Kwinter and Bruce Mau, in addition to our moderator and colleague from Communication Design, Santiago Piedrafita. For this third session, we will continue our discussion on New Architectural Mediums. Both of tonight's participants are not only deeply familiar with the debates surrounding this subject but also seem to be comfortable residing in the liminal space between those debates; they are **devotees of intermedia design** if not architecture.

While neither Bruce nor Sanford are formally trained as architects they are both deeply engaged in its discourse and in **new forms of architectural production and practice**. The decision to bring them together tonight has as much to do with their capacities to galvanize the many underpinnings of a discourse on media, mediums, and architecture as much as it does with the hope that they will sketch out a road map of ways in which we might think about media and mediums in the future.

Let's start with the idea that a book is typically seen as an **object encoded with experiences** via text and image—*not* an artifact which encapsulates a **physical, optical, and tactile experience**. **01** *Zone 6*, one of the early compilations among the internationally coveted series of books Mau designed, and which Kwinter co-edited, flipped this presumption on its head. **02** Oscillating fonts, paper types, and page number locations were among the many elements deployed to **activate** what was formerly **encrypted into a live experience**. A film flipping through the book unveils the degree to which the *Zone* books were key in suggesting how **an intermediated discourse**— design, architecture, philosophy, art criticism—and its documentation might inflect traditional design principles; and particularly architectural design. **03** While journals of a similar nature have existed, and practices between art, architecture, and philosophy are not without precedent in the early or mid-twentieth century, no finer a point, no better designed, no better edited or better curated a collection of contents and consortium of textual objects had **simultaneously offended and delighted** architects with such intense fervor as this book, and the series at large.

The pairing of our two guests then draws upon their historical collaboration as well as their **capacities as provocateurs**. Both in architecture and in their native disciplines, they are the most **productive form of an enfant terrible**. They are widely appreciated for their **utter curiosity and courage** to bring forth otherwise complex and seemingly absent ideas we should be considering; as a discourse, as a practice, and as a design-based culture.

Sanford, whose background is in comparative literature, is a **true trans-media thinker**. He is a wordsmith par excellence. His language goes beyond craftsmanship and often resonates with the poetic; evoking some sort of mysterious "phase change" moving out of the literary and across mediums. **04** His edited tomes are **as visual as they are tactile, soft, and spongy**. **05** His written work evokes **ulterior media**. They insert the **temporal,** **06** **the sonic**, **07** **the gravitational**, **08** **and the energetic** directly into the architectural. His range is astonishing, where he can enlist anything from **biological morphology** **09** to **thermodynamics,** **10** inviting architecture to **push and explore potential intermedia capacities** in its praxes.

Bruce, too, clearly takes language seriously and uses it **experimentally**. **11** While he may also transform it into the experiential, he does *not* do so in an identical way to Sanford. Through his background as a graphic designer, **12** writing, its fonts, and its graphic qualities underpin the beginnings of the myriad of ways in which Bruce so easily **traverses numerous design disciplines**, including architecture. **13** The conflation of a dot matrix as a texture **14** or of a font as something equally raster and vector **15** are only a few of the ways in which his more traditional design work, when limited to a book, already **engages the experiential**.

I suppose one of the issues on the table in this evening's session is *content*; **16** as was alluded to in the inaugural session on Mediums. If architects incorporate media into their work, the most difficult and perhaps challenging aspects of that prospect is how to give that consortium of multi-media elements form and an experience or sensibility. It is an "after geometry" type of problem that could be oriented toward **new types of content**; which could be a way of saying toward **new types of experience**. This is important to foreground in these sessions as the "New" in New Architectural Mediums has less to do with new media technologies and more to do with investigating new intellectual frameworks through which we can explore and understand, historical, contemporary and future media technologies we use as designers and architects.

The ways in which both Bruce and Sanford engage areas of

architectural design that are somewhat **taboo and turn design problems into assets** is impressive. While the origins of their work may be in their native formats—writing or graphics—they seem to have discovered ways in which those formats leak into architecture and re-center it toward **live experience**. Their work allows us to see the spaces between various mediums and between various senses as both a contemporary and future space that necessitates design and **engages architecture's urban vitality**.

We might say that the experiences we desire and which are pleasurable are anything but vacant of media. They are not spaces of **abstract "absence"** set against the cacophony of devices and stimuli we interact with on a daily basis. As Steven Johnson noted in his book *Everything That Is Bad For You Is Good For You,* when distinguishing between *Dragnet* (1951-1959) and *The Sopranos* (1999-2007) the reason someone will sit down and watch fourteen hours of television has everything to do with how you form a dense interplay of mediums. In Johnson's scenario, this has everything to do with the use of camera angles and types of cameras, lighting effects, plot line trajectories, character formations, and dialogue textures. **The more immersive the better** and **the more mediated the better**; the idea is to wander, to get **productively lost**. The trick is in how a designer balances a wide range of media and sensorial stimuli, while giving them a **collective shape** and trajectory without ever allowing any one of them to fully snap into focus or dominate—how to make everything that appears bad not only good, but both **desirable and vital**. Our guests this evening have a track record of doing just this and thus their thoughts and insights into this Pratt Session I suspect will be both enlightening and invaluable.

# Sanford Kwinter

## NEW YORK, NY

Implicit in our framework tonight is the tacit affirmation that attention to the senses is a matter of both interest and urgency for design but also for thought, for ethics, and for life. It also presupposes that existing accounts are precarious and insufficient. The problem that the "senses" poses to the historian, the philosopher, the physiologist, and ultimately to the designer is immense, almost boundless. Since we have limited time to speak about this tonight, it makes sense to abandon systematicity and to attack the problem from any perspective whatever. The senses have an important and dynamic history, and are therefore enormously fluid. The senses first and foremost constitute a framework, a set of tools that we use and continually remake according to our need and according to the structure of the reality we seek to engage.

A broad and foundational concept that I would like to affirm at the outset is the following: To every organism, there corresponds a specific and distinct universe determined by the highly particular sensory capacities proper to it. The differences we find between worlds corresponds not only to different species each adapted for a different niche, habitat or environment, but extends to each individual within a given species or even population. The individual variations increase in number and magnitude with the sophistication and complexity of the organism in question.

Differences of a remarkable scope and amplitude exist even between the nervous systems of identical twins and even Siamese twins, whose experience of the spatial environment differs as little as is physically and biologically possible between any two organisms. This attestation is based on the keystone concept of which we hear a lot today, that of *neuroplasticity*. The brain is primarily shaped not by heredity but by stimulus. Experience turns every brain into a categorically unique entity.

The principal job of the organism is to create meaning from the exterior givens that present themselves to it. The world contains not only inert resources to be discovered but also active and creative ones. This is particularly the case in the human world, which contains other unique communicative, collaborative, and creative human actors. This presumption brings us to the first point in my prospective meta-manifesto of the senses: Sensing is not only a solitary activity, it is significantly social and collective.

Humans fashion worlds according to their specific sensory endowments and make these highly particular worlds available to other humans through formal arrangements such as art, music, literature, architecture, and film.

The second affirmation of my meta-manifesto has to do with how we understand and represent to ourselves this category of sensed experience and understanding. To address this I would like to go back to a keystone work of theoretical neurobiology from the 1930s, that of Kurt Goldstein, in a book entitled *The Organism: A Holistic Approach to Biology Derived from Pathological Data in Man*. It was Goldstein's breakthrough and historical contribution that the study of functional and coherent behavior can be more effectively illuminated by the study of the disturbances to it, not its normal state. Goldstein thought about the perceiving organism as a manager of order and disorder. The bizarre symptoms that befall brain-damaged patients, their so-called pathologies, are seen not as components of the disease but rather as belong to the enduring, spontaneous, creative, and healthful life force itself, as the organism builds a functioning and orderly system to route behavior around the damage and restore a working equilibrium between internal and external environment.

The sustained task to establish and maintain a functional whole—casting of the organism as a holist project—is the work of life. It is, in sum, the work of the senses to provide the scaffold for just this action in and on the world and the self. Since, by nearly all contemporary accounts, we substantially invent the world in perception rather than simply receive it, the foundational creativity that lies at the root of human experience and sensory processing presupposes entering a "pathological" state. This non-moral approach to "pathology" is what I am advocating today from a design perspective. The lesson I wish to call attention to here is that the greatest resource and opportunity that we can derive from our senses is precisely their capacity to create syntheses that draw on what is found beyond or outside of their routine competences.

The next critical element in the meta-manifesto is the summary principle that governs all nervous system activity, to wit, *the labor of integration*. Every perception we have—whether it's within the modality of music, painting, or listening to a lecture—is an integrative process. A simple lesson that contemporary neuroscience offers us is that our senses continuously and vigorously compose and unify us as well as the world outside. Sensing is not simply a means to receive the world but rather actively *to invent it* in such a way that it can present a whole new set of possibilities through which to extract novelty and sensual, intellectual resources from it.

Where are these resources in the world? It's through the transformation and the cultivation of the senses that we would access them. Hence, the next affirmation of this meta-manifesto would invoke the theory of *affordances*. Some people, familiar with this term, may imagine it comes from the Apple corporation for the simple reason that they reputedly designed their whole user system based on the theory of affordances (the influence of Donald Norman) that was developed by the perceptual psychologist J.J. Gibson.

What Gibson tells us is that perception is not an archival process of storing images and comparing them to incoming data but rather an increasingly skillful and open-ended probing of the environment in search of points of engagement and use. Hence the definition of affordance: the point of engagement and use.

A remarkable term used by another writer, a theoretical biologist from around the same time as Goldstein, named Jakob Johann von Uexküll, in a work called *A Stroll Through the Worlds of Animals and Men* is the German term of "Tonus" to describe the flavor with which parts of the environment are able to serve the engagement and modification of the world by a sensing organism. One example is the way in which a sea anemone presents its one form in three different "use tones" to the hermit crab. Depending on what the hermit crab's disposition is at a given time, the anemone serves alternately by providing a "protective tone" when the hermit crab has lost its cover of ocean bottom flora and requires protection from predatory squid. The crab wears the anemone like a helmet on its head. When the crab has molted its shell, the anemone will take on a "dwelling tone" as the crab crawls into the anemone for shelter. And finally, if starved for several days, the anemone takes on a "feeding tone"—the anemone is configured as a thing to eat and the crab proceeds to munch on it.

The principle here is that the object is in each instance utterly transformed in relation to its tonality, and this tonality is the feature that the organism is seeking and finding. We humans are no different. Von Uexküll shows that in the course of human experience, the simple fact of accumulated cultural experience endows worldly objects with tonalities that forever become the entities sensed. The implications of these formulations are immense and go far beyond most current reductionist approaches to the senses.

The next entry in our provisional meta-manifesto concerns the problem of movement. There is no perception without movement. A thing is perceptible insofar as it achieves a form of distinction from its surround. The surround-dependence is the single most important but neglected aspect of perception studies. It reminds us however of the preeminence of context.

My final meta-manifesto point today has to do with the twin origins of sensation and thought itself. Sound and smell are both processed in the same primitive parts of the brain and hence both modalities appear to have the capacity to invoke an immensely wide set of integrated sensations through memory triggers. The sudden arrival of a scent from one's childhood can create not just the memory of the scent but of the total multidimensional experience—an almost complete psychedelic re-experiencing. Diane Ackerman, in her book *A Natural History of the Senses*, speculates that smell was the "first of our senses" and was critically deployed in the earliest sea dwelling organisms as a means of discovering food and evading predation. This olfactory apparatus, a bulb on a nerve cord, in later eons was precisely the tissue system that evolved into our poly-sensing thinking and feeling brain. Today, our essentially saltwater bodies are barely transformed vestiges of our early aquatic life systems and environments and these sensory modalities in fact have come along with them.

In closing I would like to invoke two features that point us far beyond the boundaries of conventional understanding to which our senses are wont to lead us. The first is the notion of "endogenous images"—objects of sense that were never directly sensed yet which are somehow present to memory and to extreme re-experience of pre-self past. The second is the peculiar role played by music to invoke and carry one into "non-ordinary" postures of sensing. The perception of acoustic flow organized as music, or frequently just sound, seems to permit the brain to access parts of brain memory and even matter outside the body. The implicit but agnostically-held hypothesis is that one can "re-experience" sensations from one's earliest stages of sentience, even from the period when one existed merely as a cluster of cells. Sound reception or hearing arguably takes place well before the development of the fully formed brain and, as Buddhists have long argued, is the last sensation stream to close at the end of life.

Hearing is also among the most discerning of the senses, more precise and hi-res, by an order or magnitude, than sight. Sound perception can access what lies beyond the limitations of sight dominated perception and provides an alternative matrix with which to approach the organization and understanding of space, time, and the matter-world. Indeed, it both presupposes and offers to action a universe where physical features and qualities, as well as emotions and sensations, thoughts and dreams all meld in a structurally "pathological" continuum where sensation and invention recover the infinite mystery that they possessed before our culture turned up the visible lights far too high.

# Bruce Mau

## CHICAGO, IL

I was born in Northern Canada, about six hours north of Toronto, in a severe climate. Our house was built on a rocky hillside which meant that we didn't have running water during the winter time. My job in the winter was to go to the well in the valley and to get water for the house every day. For the longest time, I didn't have any sense of how that experience was related to my life as a designer. Over time, I realized that in fact, that experience I share with about 12 percent of the world's population, about a billion people don't have access to clean water. That experience gave me an empathy for other's experiences that is central to everything that I do. The core operating system of design is empathy, the ability to understand other people's problems.

I started working before the computer was introduced in the workplace, but I saw that it was going to transform everything we do. As this thing connected to every other thing, it was going to create a transparency that had never existed before. Now everything is communicating. There's no part of the world that isn't telling a story. What you want as a brand, a business, an institution, or a government is to create the story that you want to be telling. You design everything you do to be telling that story. That's a fundamental difference in the way that we think about what design does. We saw a transition from visual style to what we call "enterprise design."

That's what *Massive Change* is committed to: helping

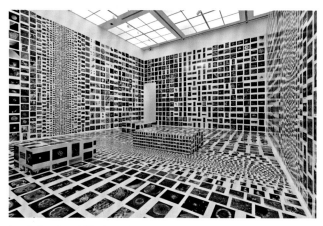

Installation view of "The Image Economy" in "Massive Change: The Future of Global Design" at the Vancouver Art Gallery, 2004

organizations, businesses, institutions, and governments to design what they do, and for that to be the story that they want to tell. We worked with folks in Saudi Arabia to design the future of Mecca. Every year, millions of people come all at once into one experience and almost every year, people get killed—just because of the design of the city. They said they wanted to do a twenty-year plan. I said, "Look, it's Mecca. Let's do a 1000-year plan and really think about the future. Let's think about the long-term and design an open system." That work is shaping my understanding of what design is capable of, and developing the practice of enterprise design. In this way of thinking, design is a leadership methodology. It's a way for people to envision a future and then systematically realize this vision.

Working on the book *Massive Change* set a new agenda for me. The back cover says it best, it's "not about the world of design; it's about the design of the world." It's about our capacity to shape the world that we experience. If you think about what's happening now, it's by far the best time in human history to be alive and working, not by a slight margin but by a radical long shot because of our capacity to solve problems. Most of the great challenges we now have are problems of success, not failure.

For the book, we studied a few hundred people who are most transformational on the planet. We set up a new institute, called the Institute without Boundaries, to do that. That project was about what we call design economies—the regions of your experience, your life that are being designed or re-designed by these new capacities. We looked at the image economy, this is like standing inside of the electromagnetic spectrum. What you see in the color images is what you would see with your naked eye, what your sensory capacity can already absorb. We've turned all the other wavelengths into an eyeball. We can use any wavelength from radio waves to gamma waves, turn it into data, turn it into visible light, and therefore be able to see it and make decisions. That's the sensory transformation that's happening.

We looked at the market—the market is not a natural space. It's a design space and how we design it determines what gets exchanged and what has value. We looked at our ability to make global decisions. If we're designing globally, we must be building global images. Finally, what we realized is that all that design is in the process of reinventing the nature and the course of wealth. We understand capital as one form. But we also know that there is wealth of information, wealth of mobility, wealth of access. There are new kinds of currencies that are being developed which provide us with a much more complex picture of wealth.

There is a new medium opportunity. We've allowed two of our sensory domains, sight and sound, to dominate our design

Installation view of "The Image Economy" in "Massive Change: The Future of Global Design" at the Vancouver Art Gallery, 2004

imagination. When it comes to the culture of architecture and design, we create and produce almost exclusively for one sense, sight. Architectural design is caged by the image. We look at architecture, we don't feel it, we don't hear it. Immersive design on the other hand has the bandwidth of reality. There are no standard formats, no existing methodologies.

We need to explore experiment and invent new formats and combinations of sensory and content engagement. To design for all the senses: start with a blindfold. The visual dominates our imagination and we need to shut it down to allow our brain to explore other possibilities. Neuroscience tells us that we are emotional decision makers, not rational spreadsheets. Use the language of passion to translate the intellectual into the emotional. Crying is a measuring stick for the quality of your work. We get a bonus if they cry.

Architects take hundreds of complex inputs and produce one coherent output. The great challenge over time is synthesis, coherence, clarity, and beauty. The ability to understand and synthesize diverse inputs across disciplines into one compelling experience is the magic and meaning of design. When we open

that space, we inspire imagination. Your work is not a fixed object or a space, it's a controlled release of information in time. If you think about what typography does, it controls the speed of information. It controls the release of content. It's a dynamic experience that evolves over time. The book is a brilliant form that allows us to sequence ideas. It allows the reader to unfold those ideas in their own experience. When we designed the first volume of *Zone*, we didn't want a book that illustrated the city. We wanted a book that behaved as a city, and had all the dynamic cultural capacity of an urban experience built into a book object.

Designers are obsessed with the user experience. We care about the individual citizen and their experience. By extension, if you care about that citizen, you care about their community because you can't have a great citizen in a toxic community. You care about their environment. You can't be a designer and not care about the impact of your work on the environment. That for me is the bottom line of what this is really all about.

Installation view of "The Image Economy" in "Massive Change: The Future of Global Design" at the Vancouver Art Gallery, 2004

Massive Change Network, One Freeman by Design

Sanford Kwinter and Bruce Mau

Biodiversity Museum: Panama Bridge of Life, designed by Frank Gehry, with
programming by Bruce Mau, 2014

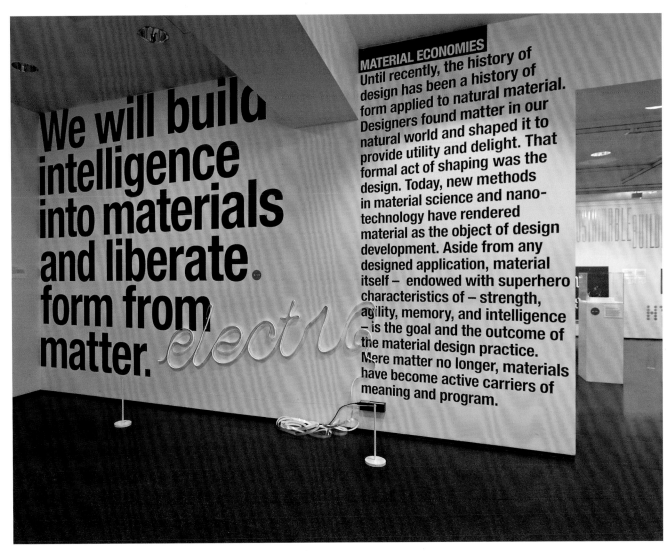

We will build intelligence into materials and liberate form from matter. *electro*

**MATERIAL ECONOMIES**

Until recently, the history of design has been a history of form applied to natural material. Designers found matter in our natural world and shaped it to provide utility and delight. That formal act of shaping was the design. Today, new methods in material science and nano-technology have rendered material as the object of design development. Aside from any designed application, material itself – endowed with superhero characteristics of – strength, agility, memory, and intelligence – is the goal and the outcome of the material design practice. Mere matter no longer, materials have become active carriers of meaning and program.

Installation view of "The Image Economy" in "Massive Change: The Future of Global Design" at the Vancouver Art Gallery, 2004

Sanford Kwinter and Bruce Mau

# Conversation

## SANFORD KWINTER AND BRUCE MAU

**Santiago Piedrafita (SP):** While Sanford was speaking, I was thinking of the dynamic and at times fragile ecosystem that develops in the balance between the individual, the community, and the larger system itself. How do you maintain that balance at a time when perhaps the individual is privileged in so many services, so many user experience designs, and in architecture? How do you privilege the balance between these components so that we return to a more harmonious whole with nature, with the built environment, and with ourselves?

**Bruce Mau (BM):** If you care for the experience of the citizen in that holistic way and you think of it as concentric rings of the citizen, the community, and ecology, there's a natural balancing. There's a natural tendency to think of it holistically. I should say that this comes from my experiences on the design council for Herman Miller. They produce almost nothing for retail; almost no individual buys their product, almost all their product is delivered to businesses. However, they obsess on the individual worker experience. By doing that, they create the most value for the businesses that they serve. It's a very productive way of understanding what our real purpose is and what our responsibilities are. I think that most designers embrace those responsibilities. It's not hard for them to do it even though the client might not be interested.

**Sanford Kwinter (SK):** That's interesting. That's how it begins. I don't have clients but I would say that those occasional people who read what I write, they have clients.

**David Erdman (DE):** Vitruvius introduced the idea of holism as aesthetic theory for beauty. If you look at the example of contemporary dramatic television, like *The Sopranos* as I mentioned, cognitive theorists and neurologists argue that the reason why people will subject themselves to that dramaturgical environment is precisely because it never comes together. You can never understand the whole. There is tension.

In the context of working with the multitude of media, stimuli, and inputs, there's also some tension between something that resolves itself and something that doesn't. Is there a new theory other than holism that can be attached to beauty? Do you think that maybe our language isn't sufficient?

**SK:** It's like saying that you're disappointed because we haven't gone beyond nature yet. There's no escape. When you talk about *The Sopranos*, you could say that it's logic. I'm trained in literature and literary structure was of great interest to us especially in the 1970s and '80s.

**DE:** I agree, but part of that is the centripetal interaction that Bruce was alluding to between the presenter and the audience. There's a way that it pulls you in. What I've read says that this is because of the gaps in between. That to my mind does not brush well with architectural theories of holism.

**SK:** Holism, or the principle behind holism, is simply that everything is connected and that everything is engaged in interaction. Interaction is what is critical. It's an open system in which anybody can slip in and fit, and isolate certain parts of the system to make them either become protective enclaves or to make them express and unfold separate effects. It means we're no longer thinking in traditional terms of a single building isolated from its environment. We begin to understand how there is a continuum of effect.

It changes how we think and that is why the acoustic or the oral is a very interesting way to reprogram, in a certain way, one's intuitions. I used to talk about the Hokulea voyages from Hawaii. Actually, Bruce and I worked on the design of *Zone 6*, which was largely based on the Polynesian navigation techniques. They did not use instruments, but the landscape to navigate the world. It was done by tapping flows, tasting the salinity of the ocean. It was done using their testicles, or they would take a pig on board. They were reading the structure of water. They were correlating all those things and they were in a constant state of alertness and improvisation. They always found the whole. The point is that Design is an ecological methodology. It's an exercise of mind and body. How do we begin to speak about the emotional aspects or the effective qualities? We know from neuroscience that there's just no escaping it.

**DE:** Would you say that's partly because it's almost falling apart? The whole system is in a potential state of catastrophe. Surfers would say that the only way you really get into a wave is by finding a space where it's almost coming apart. That's the most vivid and intense peak moment.

**SK:** Why do we say it's coming apart if it's the productive moment, if it's the opportunity?

**DE:** I just wonder if holism is the right word for that.

**BM:** If you're implying a classical sense of completion and a discrete object, I think that's not what we're talking about. The beauty that I'm referring to is a different kind of beauty.

It's a beauty of an open productive system that is accessible in new ways.

**SP:** You talk about the necessity to arrive at a total ecology that reconciles the human ecology and the natural ecology. I'm assuming that there will be a lot of wear and tear in that coming together but also great potential, great beauty. Can you talk a little bit more about the concept of total ecology, certainly as it relates to architecture, as it relates to systems, interaction user experience, but also as it relates to nature itself?

**SK:** First of all, I am utterly unembarrassed by romanticism in relation to the natural world. That permits me to do and say things that more self-conscious or intimidated academics or philosophers might not do. What is a total ecology? I remember using that phrase and thinking it meant something. What is important is to recognize and engage the part of the world that unfolds indifferently to us—the natural universe. It is the mystery from which we come, it is the mystery toward which we will return. I don't any longer think it is inaccessible to ourselves. Our bodies and our brains are

intimate products of that natural world. We can access them through what the Romans called "the movements of the soul." There is a life that we can become in touch with which connects us to these processes. If nothing else, there are lessons to be learned. I think if you do cry, that's where the crying comes from.

**SP:** I like your description of the watery context from which we came and now we embody it. We're salt and so I do understand that we have the DNA to achieve and internalize.

**SK:** It's more than DNA. It's almost the molecular relationship. Many of the great composers of the twentieth century, people like Karlheinz Stockhausen, Paul Hindemith, and even Iannis Xenakis, understood that their business was organizing the essential matter of the universe, which was vibration, and that everything was music, including the things with periodicities that were so diffuse that no single human could ever experience them; things that take 5,000 years to happen even though they keep cycling and happening again. That kind of embeddedness is the richest resource that we

Santiago Piedrafita (left), Bruce Mau (center), Sanford Kwinter (right) in conversation during Pratt Sessions 03

Sanford Kwinter and Bruce Mau

have for invention because that's what the universe does. The universe is ceaselessly inventing. You don't have to get lost in traditional terms like *holism*. What it really is, is this feeling for matter, which can be known through feeling more than through the mathematics of physics, et cetera.

**BM:** We had an extraordinary experience in Panama when we were working on the Museum of Biodiversity. We spent a day in the jungle with E.O. Wilson. We went to a place where they are researching the ecology of the place. They built a construction crane so they could get above the canopy of the trees. One of the things that E.O. Wilson said, one of my favorite quotes ever, was, "Rock is slow life and life is fast rock." Ultimately all you are is animated rock. You're a material that was formed in the core of stars and that life has a project going that doesn't care about us. We are one of millions of prototypes that it continues to innovate. In the end, all of that keeps going and we'll slide back into the earth.

In fact, once you understand that we're not separate from or above nature, you take a very different stance to what you're doing and how you're doing it. Ultimately your work is fitting into this ongoing process. We are ourselves in the process of producing that life. Life is not happening to us, our project as designers is to design it, produce it, and create the life that we imagine it can be. Ultimately, that's our opportunity but also our responsibility. For me, it's not about coherence that looks beautiful in the classical sense. It is a new kind of beauty that becomes possible when you start to see this way of being on the planet.

**DE:** What I find so compelling about that is that technology would be included in that. It's not like nature comes first, we come second, and machines come third. Somehow technology becomes part of our sensate prosthetic. There is not an essentialist or ontological distinction; they are enmeshed. Machines might precede humans and human nature in this intellectual framework.

**BM:** We know so much more than we did fifty years ago and the responsibility that comes with it is dramatic. We now know that technology fits into an ecology, and we begin to have a sense of the damage that it does. I think once we start to understand that, our responsibility as designers is fundamentally different. It's the most exciting time to be working when that starts to open up to us, when we can really see the implications of our decisions and how we're thinking about this. We can start to design the outcomes that we want, and not just allow it to be random.

**SP:** I very much appreciate that realization. We're not talking about the biological only but also everything in the social realm. When thinking about a design of an experience, certainly we are wrestling the material world and implications of those decisions but we now wrestle with orchestrating social experiences as well. You mentioned for example, the imperative necessity of distinguishing users, individuals, communities, the environment from the mere functional, the paying customer. How do we distinguish, for example, a more noble project from a mere service, a mere system that appears ecological, that appears to create a new possibility but might deliver more problems, more of the same?

**BM:** I think that we have for the most part abandoned that problem and allowed it to happen willy-nilly. We have allowed the absolute free enterprise culture to colonize our social behavior. One day we'll wake up from that nightmare and begin to actually design it and begin to push back to say, my rights as a citizen include my data and my information, my rights as a citizen include my ideas and my privacy. If you look at the Panama Papers and WikiLeaks, and the recent abdication of the rights of the citizen to their personal data being sold without their agreement or willingness—all of that is a frightening colonization of social space. Ultimately, designers are going to be the ones who have the capacity to reshape it, and we have to design new formats and structures to recover liberty in that space.

**Catherine Ingraham:** I remember the first book from *Zone* very vividly and how it had a huge impact. What I don't understand at this moment though is the collaboration between you and Sanford, because it seems to me you have described radically different relationships to the problem of experience or to the issue of experience. The potential for designing experience versus the production of experience is radically different. Maybe going back to the initial collaboration, I would love to know what happened.

**BM:** He's the problem, I'm the solution!

**SK:** Let me see if I can explain it in a friendly and discrete way. Accommodating the ends of corporate interests and let's say of the broader system's interest, we could say generally the forms of neo-capitalism, which have a lot to do with neurocapitalism, do post certain questions. What Catherine certainly is picking up is that I am asking a political question of, "What is our right to claiming our nervous system and our brains?" Not just our brains but our bodies, our senses and how we can make them produce transgressive cultural sensations, et cetera, which are not amenable to monetization or just a simple integration into the well-oiled machinery of neurocapitalism. Now, you say one day we should wake up and when we do we're ready. The question, of course, is what can we do? Because not everyone is asleep and especially today, it's an incredible moment to produce. Remember, when you had time before you were answering the phone and we were dreaming up ways to mess up the city. Oh, we invented fake news! We wanted to upset the stock market in Toronto, and we put fake news where you used to buy newspapers. There was a situationist type of militancy that is appropriate to every context. In a certain sense, we would invent our own projects to a certain degree. Even in *Zone*, we were all naïve and not worried about making a living. Bruce, you ought to start thinking about inventing some projects and being your own client.

**BM:** We are doing that.

**SK:** To make money or to make news?

**BM:** To do the right thing. Also, the idea that within the existing system, there aren't opportunities for radical transformation. We're in the process of working on a project to redesign Medicaid. Today, many people die because of the way that it's designed. I mean, I'm not interested in being transgressive in a negative way. I'm interested in being transgressive in a positive way.

**SK:** I'm not talking about negative transgression. Let me give you an example. You're still working for a client. One of the ways in which I will be wasting a lot of energy over the next year is trying to get the World Heritage Foundation to protect a hunter gatherer trance stance as a state of mind. Imagining that once a state of mind can become protected by the official bodies is that it would open the doors to a lot other states of mind that people might seek to organize and maybe to formalize and protect. Because I do feel that that is really where the great ecological disaster that is happening around us is about to happen. I'm saying again, I don't have clients but it doesn't seem to me like this is a bad time for you to invent some projects of your own, not simply do the best possible good for existing clients but to impose.

**BM:** I've never thought of it as one or the other. I've always done my projects. I used *Zone* and my clients to do my project. I don't see it as this or that. My work with Freeman is precisely that. If Freeman does 15,000 events a year, practically every health organization produces an event that brings their world together in order to advance and accelerate their efforts. For me, that's just the coolest Massive Change opportunity I could possibly hope for. Now, is it within a business context? Absolutely, but...

**SK:** The Massive Change project was something you could call a self-initiated cultural tsunami, distinct from tweaking Freeman.

**BM:** Again, for me, it's never been one or the other. I'm going to figure out how to leverage all that stuff to do the thing that I think is possible, that I think is meaningful. I want all our work to be advancing the world as best as we can, that's the bottom line.

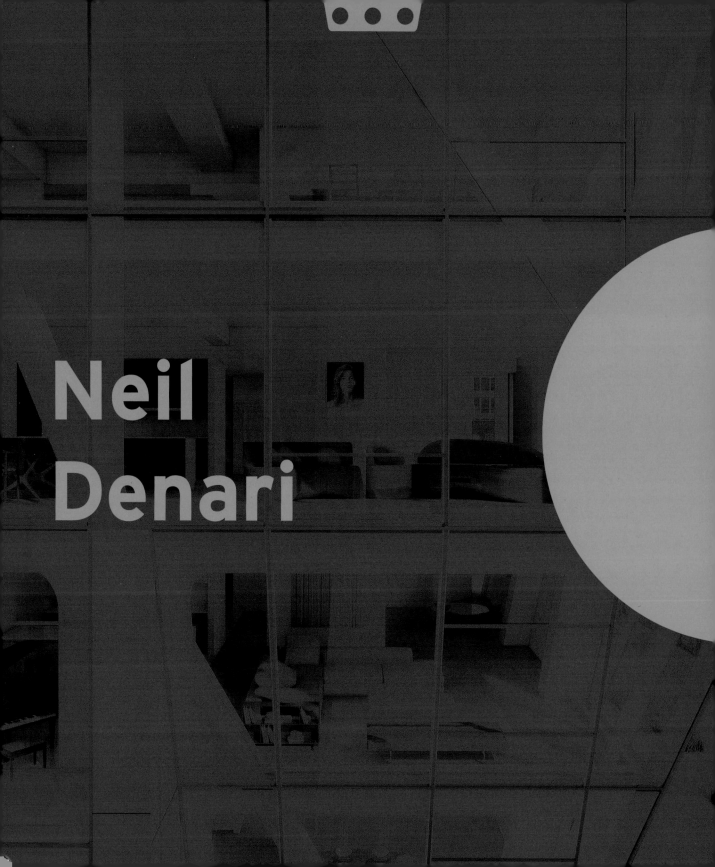

# Neil
# Denari

# Thomas Leeser

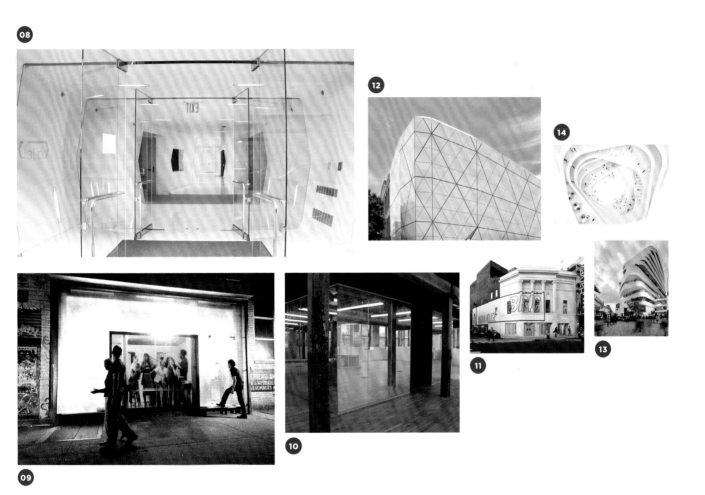

# Introduction

## DAVID ERDMAN

Tonight, Neil Denari and Thomas Leeser have come together to discuss New Architectural Mediums; continuing this thread of discussion from the Spring. Both speakers are seminal figures in the use of **representational media** and the **cultivation of "the digital"** at the end of the twentieth century.

Yet they're here tonight because the media and mediums they continue to tinker with are now in the work. They are no longer a separate abstract representational or generative aspect of their design strategies, but the graphics and the cinematic systems (for each respectively) are actually **imprinted in the work** and its **live experience**. This is significant, is explicitly **post-digital**, and might suggest two very different (yet related) ways architects can engage in an **"intermediated" architectural practice**; a subject of considerable debate in past sessions on this topic.

Neil's work is **graphic** throughout—from the desk of his studio to the completed building; let alone the esoteric graphics of his coveted and popularized drawing techniques. **01** His work is **loaded with content**—even though it may not appear that way. It's encrypted with various **interactive codes**. **02** Projects have a quasi-magnetic quality, where they collect signage, and mesh it into an architectural surface. **03** Neil's work has **exploited concepts of "the pixel**," **04** or the **hatch; 05** further **conflating architecture content and graphic content**.

Beyond this *intermedia* method, the work has a skillful interdimensional affect, shifting swiftly and elusively from 2D to 2.5D, to 3D; **06** details interact at four dimensions, repeatedly across an impressive oeuvre of completed works. **07**

If Neil's work explores the graphic, Thomas's work is an interesting counterpart; exploring the **cinematic**. This goes beyond *scripting* or a formal effect—two ways in which cinema has been prevalently depicted in architecture discourse. The **screen is literalized** in his projects, **08** turning **facades into a screenplay** of sorts. **09** He has combined **object and screen** in **synesthetic installations**. **10**

In a number of more recent works, the screen and the object two-dimensionally and four-dimensionally begin to interplay. In some of these projects, facades have a kind of op-art, **11** **black and white staccato** quality. **12** A building may appear flat at moments, and then, "pulses" into something that's three-dimensional. **13**

Increasingly, the screens in the projects have become interiorized. They set deeper, establishing a greater distance from the threshold entry where they form a kind of **object-void penetrating into mass. 14** I would argue that as this has occurred there is the collapsing of a **cinematic object** with an architectural object producing a **thickness, depth, and immersive multi-dimensional set of qualities**.

While there may be very different interests driving the work—**the cinematic** versus **the graphic**, for example, neither media nor mediums are ulterior to the architecture of either designer's thinking or work; nor are those mediums fully integrated. There is a **tense, course, semi-autonomous** relationship between them. What is key is that the medium and mediums are *not* that which leads up to the building, but they are **"in the house"** so to speak, making their work and their thinking ripe for engagement in this trajectory of the Pratt Sessions on New Architectural Mediums.

# Neil Denari

## LOS ANGELES, CA

We typically think of graphics as describing media systems, which we understand as printed or projected. But the word *graphic* has to do with things that are intense and real. We use the term to describe sex and violence in the most vivid and sometimes horrific, sometimes unseemly, sometimes ugly ways.

Based on this, I developed a law of syllogism. If the real equals the graphic, and the graphic equals the vivid, then the vivid equals real. This syllogism tries to close loops, but also tries to understand how relationships between material worlds, graphic worlds, representational worlds all feed back on themselves. In this age of media, where we all live more or less in a state of distraction, if we didn't admit that architecture was in fact historically seen as a medium as opposed to an old device to resist everything that's quicksilver in the world now, that would be a real problem.

What I'm presenting here is about architecture not being submitted to and taken over by the immaterial world but collaborating with it.

The first project I want to show is the Endeavor Screening Room from 2004. This work emerged out of the information paradigm, where we were trying to strip away rhetoric, especially architectural rhetoric, and only tell a story. The project was embedded with a geopolitical premise about the generic idea of technology being a single voice. These conceptual surfaces had to, in their constructed mode, be defined in terms of thickness. It was about being de-familiarized from a building as if you were looking at a section, as well as being immersed in space itself. Although there's graphic content here, what was of primary importance to us was that it would be built out of drywall, that it would be white, and that it would show no sense of how the hand put it together. This project was very much about using material as an abstract device.

In our HL23 project, we translated some of the same agendas into the building. An aluminum trim, which is about 18 inches wide, meets a ceramic frit of about 13 inches wide, and the black and silver frame of the curtain wall system, to articulate the form. In this project, the effects of reading structural thickness is both a modernist idea of expression, but also something well beyond that in terms of describing the project graphically. The ceramic frit is the description of the structure on the building. It tries to produce a collaboration between 2D and 3D.

I'd like to think that our work in some ways deals in aspects of immediate recognition of the legibility of form and elements that produce delayed responses. Some people operate at the

Neil M. Denari Architects, Endeavor Screening Room, Beverly Hills, CA, 2004

Neil M. Denari Architects, HL23, New York, NY, 2012

level of the graphic in which it seeks to produce immediacy via the primitive, or something that's stripped down.

Now, for a long time I thought that to talk about the collaborative nature of architecture and the graphic—the abstraction, having the building look like it's printed, having the building always painted so that it would do away with the notion of materiality and the hand—was interesting. But quite honestly, between me and you, this also limits the practice. I could push it, but I would also find dead ends.

In some respects, projects that are about masonry are not typically thought of as being able to convey the graphic. Once you do a masonry building, whether it's a brick or concrete building, you get connected to the history of architecture. Brick and concrete buildings, of course, go back to the beginning of time.

We've worked on two residential tower projects in Vancouver. One is on Broadway, which runs all the way across the city. Developers come to you and say, "Please produce something different." In our case, we might respond that the difference is going to meditate on the project of the graphic. The building is shaped by zoning, 80 feet between towers, a 100-meter height

limit, a slope in the back, which lops off an extruded mass so we don't have egregious shadows over neighboring buildings.

A slice produces a tip at the top of the building that allows a view to the two Lions, two mountain peaks that are visible from much of the city. While this project shapes a void to shape that view, it also produces another peak. Now, this building is made out of brick, which is odd in the city of glass. It's interesting to think about material convention, in this case brick, as being far away from the idea of delivering new responses to what building is, but in this case the building is completely driven by its tectonic project, and it's what I call "shape masonry."

The last project I'll present consist of two towers in a transitioning, low-rise neighborhood. First, we're dealing with the issue of the copy—these are self-similar buildings. We've produced a scale shift in the windows, by framing four units. We went so far, of course, as to work with black and white stripes and de-familiarizing the project further, but in the end, the window pattern and the window differences in the pattern do the work to produce the effects of both immediate and delayed responses.

Neil M. Denari Architects, Vancouver, Canada

Neil M. Denari Architects, L.A. Eyeworks, Los Angeles, CA, 2002

Neil M. Denari Architects, Endeavor Screening Room, Beverly Hills, CA, 2004

Neil M. Denari Architects, HL23, New York, NY, 2012

# Thomas Leeser

**BROOKLYN, NY**

When I hear the term new media, I always think about the past. In one of my first projects, I explored our strange relationship to nature and I designed a jacket made of grass. The outer layer was made of felt that was impregnated with grass seeds and underneath were two layers of metal weave, separated by a perforated film. It was kind of a forerunner to a touchpad, actually. You get different conduit responses when you move your finger over a touchpad. In the case of this jacket, when you moved your arms different electric connections were made and there was a loudspeaker and an electronic synthesizer. This was the beginning of new media for me.

I recently came across an image of a suit from the 1800s, designed for bear hunters in Siberia, that reminded me of this project and it made me realize that quite a few of my projects have been strangely similar to this one. I'm very interested in this idea of defending against external environments.

In 2007, we won a competition for the World Mammoth and Permafrost Museum in Siberia. This region has the most extreme climate in the world. In the winter, the temperatures go down to minus 50 degrees, and in summer it sometimes gets up to

90 degrees. We had to design a building that defended itself against this extreme environment. Spikes hold the building up because when the ground thaws after the harsh winter, the building would otherwise sink into the ground. At the same time the spikes on top of the building amplify sun lines and capture natural light.

A few years later we were invited in Moscow to do a competition for the Polytechnic Museum and Education Center. The site on Lenin Hills is fantastic, but it's surrounded by boring, fake Baroque contemporary developer architecture. We felt we had to defend ourselves against this boredom by designing a very aggressive building. We felt the architecture had to be provocative. We lost the competition, of course.

We did another project in Hong Kong, the West Kowloon Arts Pavilion, that for some reason also ended up with these spikes. The idea was that each of these spikes has a loudspeaker and then you have a sound cloud around it. Because it's very hot in Hong Kong, we also thought a little mist would be a nice thing.

Then, these spikes for some strange reason even made it into the Museum of the Moving Image in Queens for the theater curtain. Having found the image of the bear suit somehow made things click.

The idea of the screen and mirror was important throughout the Museum of the Moving Image. The entrance is a semi-transparent mirror; as you enter the museum, you enter the dark side of our culture. What was important for me is the idea that you break the logo or signage of the museum, to de-monumentalize the idea of a museum.

Inside, a series of leaning walls creates moving or cinematic space, as David put it in his introduction. As you move through the museum the walls sometimes look straight, sometimes they don't. We wanted the floor to do the same, so that mirrored glass folds the garden floor up and from the inside, it folds the floor down.

We designed a bar in Chelsea, which was actually called Glass. In the early days of first coming to New York, I spent a lot of time in bars and I discovered that the most important thing in bars and clubs was the bathroom; that's where everything happened. I thought, even though it's a small place, the unisex bathroom has to go into the front of the bar. You see it on the facade in blue glass, and it's a window you can see into from the outside, but inside, it just looks like a mirror. So, you have people inside putting on makeup, adjusting their bras—whatever they do—while outside people can observe all of that, and usually are intrigued to go inside.

Thomas Leeser, Electronic Grass Jacket, 1970s

Siberian Bear Hunting Armor from the 1800s

Leeser Architecture, World Mammoth and Permafrost Museum, 2007

I observed this behavior for a while. What was interesting was that people would go inside, they'd have a drink, go to the bathroom, and they would forget. They would then come outside again, and think, "Oh, shit. What did I..?" It shows that people can have very little awareness of their environment.

We've been working with the City of New York for many years on the aquarium for the New York Zoo. It is a very small space, where we proposed four tanks in the corners of the room. Behind the fish tank you have a one-way mirror. When you stand in front of the fish tank you feel like you are actually in the water; the mirror puts you behind the fish in the water, so you become just as much an object on display as the fish. In addition to the mirror, we have a camera with motion sensors that track the fish and present information about the fish behind the glass. It's sort of like augmented reality, but it's on video walls. Then, of course, you can download this information on your phone.

Another project we did here in New York was for the Paley Center, the former Museum of Broadcasting and Television. They have an archive of almost every television show that was ever broadcast and they didn't know how to allow access to visitors. We proposed robotic monitors that would talk to you. They would approach you, they would ask you a question, and you could ask the robots questions in return. These robots would act as casual access to the very complicated archive of television, film, and video.

The last important aspect in our work is cuts. Architects are always obsessed with sections, because they seem to show everything. Architects are also always obsessed with the human body—from Le Corbusier's Modulor to Da Vinci's Vitruvian Man. I thought I'd do my own man and that it would be most interesting to see section cuts of the human body. Especially a moving section reveals how dense and intense our interiors are. We did a proposal for an exhibition in Grand Central Terminal in 2003, and a video version of this moving section that will be in the 2018 Venice Architecture Biennale. Here it is flattening a 3D scan, as we move around. It creates this strange unfolding of space and object.

Leeser Architecture, Hong Kong Art Pavilion, Hong Kong, 2014

Leeser Architecture, Moscow Polytechnic Museum and Education Center,
Moscow, Russia, 2013

Leeser Architecture, Museum of the Moving Image, Queens, NY, 2011

Leeser Architecture, Glass Bar, New York, NY, 2002

# Conversation

## NEIL DENARI AND THOMAS LEESER

**David Erdman (DE):** I'm glad that Neil started his presentation discussing the word *graphic* as relating to intensity, and that Thomas began with an image of defense. When we typically think of media, we think about the Apple gestalt—it's passive and comfortable, but if we look at the legacy of intermedia, from James Turrell to NASA, it presents a very different aesthetic about how we use media. Does it have anything to do with pleasing and making it comfortably inhabitable?

**Neil Denari (ND):** I'm interested in humanity but not in the sense that architecture would cease to make someone think. It's interesting to look at Thomas's spike projects and issues of defense, because it depends on what you do with it. In the case of the spiky suit, the wearer is just trying to survive against the bear. The other side of the coin is something outwardly aggressive in terms of those references. For me, I'm trying to understand how the upright body, the grid, orientation, and equilibrium can be shifted in a way that carries on an avant-garde project, but does so with less energy. In 1996, we did an installation at Gallery Ma in Tokyo. When the owner of the gallery walked in, he said, "I don't know what this is, it's completely foreign to me, but I feel comfortable."

**Thomas Leeser (TL):** Comfort is the last thing I'm interested in. I think architecture shouldn't be comfort. I just got rid of my Le Corbusier couch because I couldn't stand sitting on the damn thing—it was so uncomfortable and I should have actually kept it for that reason. Comfort is most often a deadening thing. Now, if somebody says they feel comfortable it in a space, it could also mean they just find it inspiring. It's about seeing the world differently through architecture. The spiky buildings are not intended to be aggressive towards people. They're against deadening environments. It's about designing something to make you ask, "What is this?" It provokes people to become more aware of where they are.

**DE:** If you talk with an interaction or software designer, a lot of what they talk about in terms of duration and playfulness is hitting many different modalities of interaction simultaneously, so that it productively confuses users into sustaining an interaction. Where are the limits of how you're using media? If the use of media itself isn't the important part—the fact that you're using robots, fog, fonts, or graphics—then what are the limits that are driving the live experience? I suspect it might be a balance of comfort and discomfort?

**ND:** In his films, Jean-Luc Godard used jump cuts to eliminate unnecessary time; to be able to quickly get from one event to another. Its sense of expediency produced a new moment in film, which was both jarring, but also oddly economical and didactic. For me, because our work is so geometrically and tectonically driven—and I would say it's much less interactive than Thomas's work in terms of engaging somebody ergonomically—we engage people primarily visually. I'm very much willing to exploit a sense of discomfort at the level of the optical. I would say that's a humane project because you're not asking somebody to behave differently, but to see and think differently.

**DE:** You could say media is immaterial and it's atectonic; you could possibly even go so far as to say it's anti-aesthetic. The designer no longer gives it the aesthetic that one might in traditional tectonics and material form. Is that the direction either of you are going?

**TL:** Well, architecture is about experience, and technology is also. In different ways, but architecture and technology can go hand in hand.

**DE:** Do you think that means it's without geometry or without aesthetic?

**TL:** No. Experience is an aesthetic. Whether it's audible only or whether it's visual, there is a very clear aesthetic to that experience.

**ND:** My answers is quite a bit conditioned by how our office is working now—more than half the work is a developer project. The program has to operate within that format, at least, financially, while still producing something different. This doesn't necessarily set up "different" as a spectacle. I would say that the level of "the same" in the world has risen to a higher level of exotic species, what I call "global generics." But it remains a challenge and a problem to be interested enough in the conditions and conventions of something like geometry, which is now directly related to constraint and freedom in terms of program. Where we don't have an apartment, we can make a trapezoidal window, and where we do, we can make a rectangular window. Those things end up serving as coded messages as to what the program or the project is doing, more than simply treating it like sculpture. In our case, I never thought what we did was as out there to the point where we'd have to say, "We're not going to do that anymore. It's an anti-aesthetic project."

**DE:** I think it's a different way of seeing and understanding aesthetics. Theodor Adorno wrote about the introduction of vinyl to the music industry and the fear that mechanical reproduction would kill live performance. From my recollection of his essay, he cites the early days of vinyl, when you had musicians like Louis Armstrong, who had an extroverted, over-performing, and over-gesticulating style for recording. I would call this a centrifugal aesthetic, if you will. It was reaching out of the vinyl to grab the audience. As that recording technology matured, you started to see performers like Van Morrison, who turned his back to the audience in live performance and whispered into the microphone. Aspects that were equally criticized for the experience of the concert (too introverted) as they were critically hailed (by Adorno in particular) as being born out of the medium of reproduction. The intimacy of his work was designed for vinyl and you only fully understand it when listening to it through that medium.

Similarly, in early stages of your careers you can see the media very much on the exterior of your projects. As your work and use of multiple media has both widened and matured, it seems one commonality emerging between projects from both firms is the use of media that is more subtle; pulling the subject into those spaces balancing geometry and media; perhaps a more "centripetal" sensibility? That is a very different aesthetic than one that puts media on the front as a "sign."

In this highly-mediated world, we can't have the same language to describe the aesthetics that we might have had through the conventions of how we would describe them geometrically and historically—requiring new terms and ideas to emerge. This is central to the Pratt Sessions where New Architectural Media is really new intellectual frameworks for considering current and future technologies more than an obsession with the media itself. So these terms and frameworks for aesthetics and sensibilities would be key distinguishing factors to advance discourse and practice.

**ND:** If we are to do architecture that neither silently lets

everything happen as substrate in the background nor screams for our undivided attention, it leaves an incredibly big zone in between for other ways in which architecture can collaborate with media. I'm still committed in an old-fashioned way to visual and optical ways in which space and the effects of space are important.

**Catherine Ingraham:** Do you think that media is capturing something of the role of ornament in prior epochs? Ornament took on communicative power and was applied in a certain sense to block out the building with its distracting narratives. Is the media that we have now also trying to cloak the building?

**ND:** Depending on its relation in architecture to other media, ornament has always either provided more content or beauty and distraction. Louis Sullivan's ornament was different than Roman ornament in terms of what it "said."

**Audience question, student**: Both of your work brings up questions of interactivity. I'm wondering how these different threads that you are taking on with the adaption of media and architecture would play out in urban public spaces like Times Square, where you would be dealing with constant competitions for attention from both virtual and physical spaces?

**TL:** Well, a place like Times Square is all advertising, but to me that's not interesting in terms of media. In the Paley Center for Museum Broadcasting and Television, technology would allow you to access information that is otherwise not visibly with you. It's not just media for media's sake. If I were asked to design something in Times Square, I would probably switch all the screens into the same color, deleting the overload of useless information. I think the danger with media is that it's easily corruptible.

**ND:** Times Square was developed before the cell phone and at that time, it was the only spectacle cities had. I don't want to abdicate the possibility that architecture could in its old-fashioned sense communicate something of difference but these days, I could see a philosophy by which an architect would say, "All I need to design is the most beautiful substrate, because most people are looking at their phones all the time." Quite honestly, it makes having an architectural project now more volatile. It's a vexing set of problems. I think for every architect, especially for students, these questions have to be driving the agendas right now.

Image of Neil Denari (left), David Erdman (center), and Thomas Leeser (right) in conversation at Pratt Sessions 05

# Overview

# Dean's Note

**TOM HANRAHAN**
**DEAN OF THE SCHOOL OF ARCHITECTURE**

*Pratt Sessions* is a new publication developed by the Graduate Architecture and Urban Design programs in Pratt Institute's School of Architecture. The school has long been host to a series of innovative publications that not only introduced readers to emerging ideas in architecture and design but presented them in new and experimental forms. Over three decades the *Pratt Journal, In Process* and *TARP* have expanded the boundaries of theoretical, visual, and topical design journals. *Pratt Sessions* joins this distinctive group with its own inventive format, and rich array of completed work and theoretical speculations by some of the most important architects and designers practicing today.

Each section of *Pratt Sessions* is a transcribed public conversation between paired designers and architects, augmented by examples of their work and observations and questions by moderator and chair of Graduate Architecture and Urban Design David Erdman. The results are provocative and unexpected and provide insights into architecture and design that are not always revealed in more traditional lecture formats. Some of these conversations demonstrate broad agreement on critical ideas in design, while others illustrate the unique differences in approach and thinking from this exceptionally talented group of contributors. All of them touch on the most important issues affecting the design of spaces, buildings, and cities today. Together they illustrate the remarkable range and complexity of thought that can be found in today's design world.

# Introduction

**DAVID ERDMAN**
**CHAIRPERSON, ASSOCIATE PROFESSOR**
**GRADUATE ARCHITECTURE + URBAN DESIGN**

In surfing, a "session" is a period in which you make something out of nothing. A moment of precision, in which one reads, galvanizes, exploits, and interacts with a consortium of forces. It is as euphoric as it is fleeting, as mysterious as it is understood. Surfers spend their lives craving a good session.

The musical equivalent is not so different. Often unpaid, informal gatherings harnessing live performance or improvised recording, one could argue that a good musical session (if witnessed or documented) is the engine behind a musician's growth. Be it musician to musician, human to aquatic medium or architect to architect, the spirit of the Pratt Sessions is to debate, question and discuss matters on the periphery and core of our discipline. To capture a fleeting moment with some precision and allow it to alter, shift, and transform dynamically.

Dean Tom Hanrahan and I have conceived the Pratt Sessions as a distributed symposium focused on two parallel research subjects we are currently examining at in the Graduate Architecture and Urban Design programs; Architectural Mediums and Architectural Contexts. Like a surfing session, these sessions are meant to galvanize something out of subtle aberrations, to read the surface closely, to gain an understanding of its depths, and to have an improvisational one-off quality; each discussion being different and having to negotiate the particularities of that specific event and its participants.

Bringing together pairings of designers and thinkers, one of whom is regional and the other non-regional (predominately from New York City and Los Angeles), the sessions curb stereotypes and assumptions about the thermohaline circulation of architecture discourse; I am here borrowing heavily from surfology, using the term for oceanic swells and current flows as an analogy for the formation of the Kittler-like discourse networks in architecture. Thermohaline circulation, or THC as it is otherwise known, has the added benefit of further deepening an allusion to the euphoria associated with titillating and redistributing those networks, which is important to the Pratt Sessions.

The circuitry of architecture discourse has been in an East to Westward flow in North America, since its instantiation in the late nineteenth and early twentieth century, and reinscribed and stabilized through the mid- and late twentieth century. One could chart this as Ivy to Prairie to the Wild Wild West. The intellectual culture of architecture with its flows and establishments thus re-inscribe Manifest Destiny often with a pejorative set of associated overtones: the East is where you think about it and the West is where you just do it! Laid back versus uptight, sunny versus cloudy, the climatological and cultural overtones continued to segregate and divide East and West Coast cultures and discourse networks until the late twentieth century when they began to reverse.

The mechanics of these established modalities of thinking, intellectual culture, and lifestyle are shifting. We feel this acutely here at Pratt – located in a primary cultural hub in Brooklyn. Back flows, ebbs, and reversals of discourse and influence can be seen across the East Coast, even seeping back into Europe where West is now influencing East. Just look at how many teachers, deans, and chairs on the East Coast are former West Coast faculty and vice versa. The curatorial approach of the sessions was to both recognize the established and historical circuitry of discourse while trying to entangle and identify its reversals and ambiguities. The sessions became an immediate and swift way to gauge the degree to which those stereotypes reassert themselves and measure where they fall apart; using the subjects of mediums and contexts as an instigator to fuel the fire.

The participants in the sessions are curated as much for their similarities as they often are for their differences. They are asked to focus short presentations on the given subject as a means of enriching a precise discourse and (perhaps most importantly) to foster student discussion; a central factor in the origins of the series. The discussions have extended for hours after presentations completed and are all followed by continued debate and discussion during the reception and Pop-Up Exhibition, including work from two artists the participants have nominated. The artist inclusions often further enriched the discourse and potential affiliations with subjects and other discourse networks—bearing the fruits of being housed within an art, architecture, and design institute such as Pratt.

My job as the Introducer of these events has been not so much to laud my esteemed colleagues (which would be easy and perhaps in line with the traditional introduction) nor account for their work in a manner accurate to either their writing or others' writings about their work. Instead it has been to give their work a narrow reading in relation to the theme at hand. I see my introductions, included here with the presentations and conversations, as one part warm up band—priming the arena for the main act—and one part having a productively oblique relationship to what the presenters may or may not show; which was often not known in advance.

This first volume of Pratt Sessions collects six sessions, three focused on each subject, involving fourteen participants, spanning one year. While each section is presented chronologically within the two subjects, they are not in the exact order in which they occurred over the course of the year. The subjects and lectures were "interdigitated," allowing for a switching from one subject to the other to unfold over the semester and year. This produced a rich texture of thinking, a range of opinions, and a productively selective amnesia about the subjects at hand. A distinct advantage to distributing a symposium and/or discussion with this type of structure is its redundancies and bifurcations.

The book design is multi-axial in response, using different page orientations—front, back, portrait, and landscape—to coalesce. This was the graphic counterpart to infusing the book with productive yet coarse mixtures of readings with the hope that one might flip between all three sections, and discover this introduction, for example, well after reading other portions of the book. The middle section of this volume collects the proper "front" of the book; now dislocated to the center and in a different page orientation. It gathers introductory material, including the essay by Catherine Ingraham, introduction by Tom Hanrahan, and the Pop-Up Exhibition artists and artworks. The two sessions sections are mirrored, forming a palindromic structure that allows for reading in two directions. They include the introductions I delivered as well as the edited versions of the participants' presentations and the conversations that followed. The book is designed to enable the reader to experience and navigate multiple sessions, browsing and "surfing" between subjects, introductions, and presentations.

This first collection owes a great deal to its participants who willingly dove into somewhat unpredictable territory. It is my opinion that it is within this zone of the session that we are the most aware and engaged. It is when those flows switch and reverse, open up counterintuitive readings and understandings that one might find a trajectory through the discourse valuable to his or her own work, thinking, or studies.

# Seeing and Articulating

**CATHERINE INGRAHAM, PH.D.**
**PROFESSOR, ARCHITECTURAL HISTORY & THEORY**
AUTHOR , *ARCHITECTURE AND THE BURDENS OF LINEARITY*

The word "media" has one definition whereas "medium" has at least thirteen definitions. Media refers to acts of communication. Medium is the milieu or environment or apparatus in which and through which communication takes place. A medium of growth, for example, allows for cellular communication. A psychic medium affords communication with the non-visible. Joshua Bolchover and John Lin (RUF)—who participated in Pratt Sessions 04—directed the 2017 Studio of Experiments in the Master of Architecture program in Graduate Architecture and Urban Design (GAUD) where they asked students to gather extensive experiential and quantifiable data about a landscape and then to de-territorialize this data into a recomposed panorama. The panoramic image became a medium that altered discussions about normative contexts such as the continuity of rural and urban landscapes. It also questioned the stability of our perceptions and the reliability of data. Contexts were rendered, in this project, as malleable.

The run-up to what we now call media, mediums and contexts has been happening for a long time—decades or centuries depending on how we position this subject matter. The concept of context, however, which is equivalent to framing, is usually understood in architecture in a fairly narrow sense. Architectural modernism claimed to repudiate contextualism, which stood for the immediate past, while architectural post-modernism claimed to restore contexts, which stood for classicism. Both movements were realized inside frameworks. Framing is what Foucault called the table of operation that makes it possible to both see and articulate the world in a particular way. What can be organized as a discourse is as crucial as what can be seen. Prior to the eighteenth-century in France, generally speaking, tables of operation did not allow people to see or articulate the meaning of fossilized bones that had been lying on the ground for millions of years. The Enlightenment figuratively shed light on these fossils in such a way that a new table of operation emerged that afforded the reinvention of human beings as *homo sapiens*. Such frameworks are epistemic fields, in other words, the specific forms that knowledge takes at any given time, and architecture, no less than the sciences and humanities, is both implicated and instrumental in the creation of epistemic fields. Since I just broached the subject of our past as living beings, this might be the place to remind ourselves that from the moment humans stood upright, which liberated our hands and head from the ground (as the paleontologist Andre Leroi-Gourhan argued in his book *Gesture and Speech*), technological evolution has accompanied our biological evolution. For some time, however, we have been arguing about what this means. Bernard Stiegler, who founded the Institute de recherché et d'innovation at the Centre Georges-Pompidou, specifically mapped this evolution in his 2009, two-volume book, *Technics and Time*. Stiegler points to the increase of speed in technological evolution in relation to biological evolution and the manner in which technologies store human memory. It seems not too obvious to say here that the discipline and practice of architecture is a field of knowledge that explores—mediates, media-izes, contextualizes, and acts as a medium for—multiple relationships between human beings and technologies, generic and non-generic *modulars* notwithstanding. And this confirms not only what we already expect of architecture—its commitment to visual and tactile elaboration—but also what we don't expect, its commitment to the symbolic.

Media, mediums, and contexts concern the technics of representation that accompany architectural work: computing, measuring, drawing, diagramming, writing, scanning, filming, recording, and translating. And they also concern apparatuses: equipment, instruments, milieus, institutions, spaces. Architects routinely revisit the central paradoxes of architecture as an intellectual-material practice and a techno-artistic discipline. All sides of these dialectics are forms of mediation: material is a medium for ideas and ideas are a medium for material; technology is a medium for art and art is a medium for technology. There have been periods when architectural history and theory have demanded that one or the other side of these co-mediations be subordinated to the other. Material, empiricists have argued, is concrete and the concrete necessarily precedes ideas. Idealists, since Kant, do not deny the existence of materiality, but they argue that we can make nothing of materiality without ideas. We are currently in a period where aspects of architectural buildings are seen as cultural techniques that oscillate, in Bernhard Siegert's words, between codes (*Nomas*, laws) and spaces (*Topos*): "Thus space and codes shift against each other in a permanently historical way."

he writes.[1] In other ways, intensification of our long-standing architectural interest in objects is, once again, leading us into object ontologies that are perilously close to fetishizing what we design and produce: doors, windows, hallways, ramps, stairs, infrastructures, aesthetic shapes and forms, organizations, landscapes.

Significant ground was laid for these discussions by Robin Evans, in his 1978 essay "Figures, Doors and Passages,"[2] and, in 1996, Beatriz Colomina's book, *Privacy and Publicity*, which articulated how modernist architecture—specifically Le Corbusier and Adolf Loos—captured cinematic and photographic techniques in spaces and windows that ushered architecture into its future role as a celebrity publicist of private life. Colomina points to the strip windows of Le Corbusier's Villa Savoye and Loos' theatrical domestic space as spectral devices that bring the occupant's gaze, and architectural spaces themselves, into recursive performative modalities.[3] Le Corbusier used the reflectivity and conductivity of glass and space to mediate perception in the Villa Savoye. Computationally articulated walls in contemporary structures—such as the Broad Museum in Los Angeles—now register multiple forms of interaction between outside and inside. Case Study houses, with their L-shaped plans, also tracked our attention from the living room to the carport as a reflection on how interiority is created by exteriority.

Contemporary architects, many of whom came through the steep learning curve posed by digital architecture in the 1990s (which seemed to promise a release from conventional authorship through automatic iterative design processes) graduated from their training about five years ago into more hybridized mediations. This, in turn, has spawned renewed interest in certain periods of architectural history, such as the Renaissance and Surrealism, which should not be mistaken, however, for a neo-classical interest.

In certain hands, the hands of Elizabeth Diller and Ric Scofidio, for example, who designed the Broad Museum, many aspects of media and contexts as political and social apparatuses that govern our privacy and the subjectivity of our public selves have been articulated in architectural terms. Through their work, we have been led to see the ways in which architecture can reveal the latency of our cultural and sentient existence. Diller, whose participation in Pratt Sessions 09 will be included in Volume 2 of this publication series, has called architecture a medium and a device that can serve, inhibit or inform our passage through it. Unlike our current desire for architectural entertainment, Diller Scofidio + Renfro do not offer effect-laden fun houses. Another forerunner, Toyo Ito, in the Mediatheque, seems, by comparison, to argue for a strictly architectural approach to media. Media, Ito implies, can be announced on the interior or exterior

walls of a building but the architectural uptake of communication, in the spirit of cybernetics, should pass through its structure—distortions or treatments of columns and windows. Ito wished to capture the multiple mediations of energy that constitute cultural spaces in order to understand a building as a thermodynamic machine.

The current distributive power of images on the internet is, of course, where we often end up in these conversations. The shifting character of the image itself—its proliferation and its facile production—is now at stake in any reflective study of media, mediums, contexts. What is the evidentiary status of an image now? Is it still constitutive of what can be seen and what can be articulated? The almost unavoidable curation of images, once placed in any kind of frame, is now capable of an infinity of manifestations and an erasure of referents. Images, as many have said, are a central form of social communication, but what kind of conversation is it? People visiting "sights" such as the Grand Canyon, stand on the edge of the sublime taking pictures of themselves. These selves are not Kantian selves insofar as these images do not stand for a transaction between nature and self. They stand as surrogates for a passive attendance at some already fully documented and known event. The Aggregate History Collective—a new generation of critical architectural scholars—are mapping, to some degree, paradigmatic shifts that culture seems to be making from representation to presentation. This is understood to be a crisis, and also a loss, of epistemic frameworks that have ordered knowledge in the context of modernity. Thus, at stake, in questions about media, mediums and contexts, is nothing less than the persuasiveness of our scientific paradigms, the existence of Nature with a large "N," nature with a small "n," the socio-political modelling of intelligence and knowledge, the meaning of history, the significance of language and seeing, the logics of capitalism, the fate of cities, the implications of ubiquitous computation, and questions of privacy and identity. An image of the environment is what the environment is. The map is the territory. All of which is of utmost importance in our disciplinary and practical relation to the richly texture worlds that are the object of our studies and the site of our interventions. Pratt Sessions creates an intensified climate for inquiry into both contemporary architectural work and critical frameworks, inherited and new.

[1] Bernard Siegert, Tr. John Durham Peters, "Doors: On the Materiality of the Symbolic," in *Grey Room* (Cambridge: MIT Press, 2012) Volume -/Issue 47/ Spring 2012, p. 12.

[2] Robin Evans, *Translations from Drawing to Building and Other Essays* (Cambridge, MIT Press, 1997).

[3] Beatriz Colomina, *Privacy and Publicity: Modern Architecture as Mass Media* (Cambridge: MIT Press, 1996).

Born in Rosario, Argentina, Marcelo Spina is an internationally renowned architect and educator. Along with partner Georgina Huljich, he is one of the principals of P-A-T-T-E-R-N-S, an award-winning critically acclaimed architectural practice based in Los Angeles with a well-established design presence worldwide. The firm brings a progressive approach to projects across scales, agendas, and geographies, insisting on the cultural and social relevance of architectural form and aesthetics in the contemporary city.

Marcelo is a licensed architect in Argentina and in the United States. He received his BArch from the National University of Rosario, Argentina in 1994, and a MArch from Columbia University, New York in 1997. He has been a design faculty at SCI-Arc since 2001 where he is also the coordinator of the Architectural Technologies Postgraduate Program. He has been a visiting professor at the Universities of Yale, Syracuse, Harvard, Berkeley, Vienna, Innsbruck, and Di Tella among others. Awards include local and national AIA awards, Architect of the Year (Third Prize, 2003), Architectural League's Emerging Voices (2012), and the prestigious USA Artists Fellowship (2013). He is the Co-Author of *Embedded* [ACDCU, 2010], co-editor of *Material Beyond Materials* (SCI-Arc 2012), and co-curator of *"Matters of Sensation"* at Artists Space [2008]. His work has been published and exhibited widely and Spina has given more than 100 lectures around the world.

# Marcelo Spina

# Eric Höweler

Eric Höweler AIA, LEED AP is a registered architect with over twenty years of experience in practice. He received a Bachelor of Architecture and a Masters of Architecture from Cornell University.

He is a principal of Höweler + Yoon Architecture. HYA is a multidisciplinary practice working between architecture, art, and media. Their multi-disciplinary projects include architecture, interactive environments, interiors, installations, furniture, concept clothing, and artist books. They embrace all scales as an opportunity to engage design research to investigate the relationships between form/performance, interactivity/media, and inhabitation/event. HYA's work is the subject of a monograph entitled *Expanded Practice, Howeler + Yoon Architecture / MY Studio*, published by Princeton Architectural Press in 2009. Awarded the Architecture League's Emerging Voices award for 2007 and Architectural Record's Design Vanguard for 2007, their interactive architecture / landscape projects were featured in the 2006 National Design Triennial at the Cooper Hewitt in New York and the Institute of Contemporary Art in Boston. Their work has been included in exhibitions at the Los Angeles Museum of Contemporary Art, the Museum of Modern Art in New York, and the Museum of Contemporary Art in Chicago. Their work has been published and reviewed in *Architect, Architectural Record, Domus, Interior Design, Architectural Lighting* and *I.D. Magazine, The New York Times, The Boston Globe, The Financial Times* and published in the following books: *Light Color Sound, Sensory Effects in Contemporary Architecture* (Norton, 2010), *Utopia Forever* (Gestalten 2010), *Small Scale, Creative Solutions for Better City Living* (Princeton Architectural Press 2010), *1000X Architecture of the Americas* (Verlagshaus Braun 2008), *Provisional Practices—Emerging Modes of Architectural Practice USA* (Princeton Architectural Press 2008), and *Young Architects Americas* (DAAB 2007).

He is currently associate professor at the Harvard Graduate School of Design. Prior to forming Höweler + Yoon Architecture, Eric was a senior designer at Diller + Scofidio where he worked on the Institute of Contemporary Art in Boston and the Juilliard School/Lincoln Center in New York. As an associate principal at Kohn Pedersen Fox Associates, Eric acted as the senior designer on the 118-story ICC Tower in Hong Kong.

Bruce Mau serves as chief design officer of Freeman, and is the co-founder and chief executive officer of Massive Change Network (MCN), a global design consultancy based in Chicago.

The work of the Canadian-born designer, innovator, visionary, and author has been dedicated to applying the power of design to transforming the world. Informed by three decades of design studio experience and collaborations with many of the world's leading artists and architects, cultural institutions, and global companies, Mau has evolved his own design thinking methodology to inspire innovative solutions to challenges in any field or environment and on any scale.

Mau has written and/or designed more than 200 books, including the landmark architecture title, *S,M,L,XL*, in collaboration with Rem Koolhaas; *Massive Change* and *Life Style*, both published by Phaidon; and the celebrated series, *Zone Books*. Mau's "*Incomplete Manifesto for Growth*," a forty-three-point statement of his thinking on creativity practice, has been translated into more than fifteen languages and shared widely on the Internet for nearly twenty years.

Among the many distinguished honors and awards bestowed on Mau are the Cooper Hewitt Design Mind National Design Award; the Philadelphia Museum of Art Collab Award; the Global Creative Leadership Award from the Louise Blouin Foundation, and the AIGA Gold Medal for Communication Design. Mau was named the Bill and Stephanie Sick Distinguished Fellow at Segal Design Institute, Robert R. McCormick School of Engineering and Applied Science, Northwestern University in Evanston, Illinois.

# Bruce Mau

Sanford Kwinter is Professor of Science and Design at the School of Architecture at Pratt Institute in New York. He is a t— who has written widely on problems of knowledge and desig— and aesthetics, as well as on the structure and evolution of cit— current interests and work deal with problems of perception, consciousness in relation to both spatial and temporal form.

He formerly served as an associate professor at Rice Unive— has taught at MIT, Columbia University, Cornell University, and University.

Kwinter has a PhD (1989) from Columbia University in Com— Literature with a dissertation entitled *Immanence and Event i— Modernist Culture.*

In 1985, he co-founded the independent publishing compa— Books with designer Bruce Mau, and theorist Jonathan Crary.

Thomas Leeser is internationally known for his iconic architectural designs at all scales. As principal of his own firm for the past thirty years, his passion for the fusion of emerging technologies and architecture has driven many of the firm's award winning designs. Thomas's commitment to architecture extends beyond practicing in the field. For the past thirty years, he has been an architecture professor at Pratt Institute, Cornell University, Harvard University, The Cooper Union, Columbia University, Parsons School of Design, Rensselaer Polytechnic Institute, Illinois Institute of Technology, and Princeton University. He is currently teaching at Pratt Institute. In his teaching and professional work, Thomas explores his commitment to innovation and the advancement of the field of architecture. Thomas specializes in museums, theaters, broadcast and educational facilities.

# Thomas Leeser

# Neil Denari

Neil Denari is principal of Neil M. Denari Architects / NMDA and a professor in the Department of Architecture and Urban Design at UCLA. His academic research focuses on urban morphology, utopias, and vivid tectonics. He received his Bachelor of Architecture from the University of Houston in 1980 and a Master of Architecture from Harvard University in 1982. Among his many awards is the 2011 Los Angeles AIA Gold Medal. Denari's work has been included in many exhibitions, including the traveling solo show "Displaced Buildings in Aperiodic City," which was inaugurated in 2017 by the T-Space Gallery in Rhinebeck, New York. His work is permanently held by eight major museums around the world. With NMDA, Denari works on building projects in North America, Europe, and Asia. In 2012, NMDA won first prize in the New Keelung Harbor Service Building competition. Denari lectures worldwide and has been a visiting professor at Harvard, Princeton, Columbia, Penn, and Rice, among other schools. He is the author of *Interrupted Projections* (1996), *Gyroscopic Horizons* (1999), and *MASS X*, forthcoming in May 2018.

Santiago Piedrafita presently heads the Graduate Communications and Package Design Department in the School of Design at Pratt Institute, New York. Previously he chaired the Department of Graphic Design and Industrial Design at North Carolina State University (NCSU). Before then the Design Department at Minneapolis College of Art and Design (MCAD).

Before joining academia, Piedrafita was Senior Designer at the Walker Art Center's Design Department, having worked with Directors Andrew Blauvelt and Laurie Haycock-Makela, respectively. At the Walker, he designed a diverse array of exhibitions, communications, and publications for the museum's multidisciplinary curatorial and institutional departments. In New York, Piedrafita worked in renowned studios such as the Museum of Modern Art's (MoMA) in-house Design Department, J. Abbott Miller's Design/Writing/Research (then joining Pentagram), and Chermayeff & Geismar Inc. (now Chermayeff & Geismar & Haviv).

# Santiago Piedrafita

# Pop-Up Exhibitions

In Fall 2017, the second semester of the Pratt Sessions series, we developed the idea to associate a Pop-Up Exhibition with each session; thanks to the suggestion of one of our younger faculty members who has taken on the role of our Special Projects Coordinator. As a graduate program, in an architecture school that is part of a larger art and design institute with vibrant departments of fine art, communications and industrial design, we thought it would be prudent to use the sessions to engage audiences in those related disciplines and praxes. Their works are reproduced and projected forming a point of interest and extended opportunity for debate and query during our post-session receptions; now fully instituted for every session. Pop-Up Exhibitions and artists for sessions that occurred prior to the commencement of this initiative were retrospectively selected and are included here.

Each participant has nominated an artist whose work they find compelling and related to both the subject at hand (Mediums or Contexts) and their individual work and/or interests. The specific works included in this book (and in the live exhibitions) may have been chosen by the participant, the artist or the editors of this book. Each artist and/or their representatives were involved in the process of selection where (to our pleasant surprise and on very short notice) all were receptive, supportive, often engaging us directly and often attending the sessions.

The curatorial trajectory of such a broad and open-ended initiative has a productive looseness that allows us to expand into and include other disciplines in the sessions. Some of the session participants incite the artists directly and they are all introduced in David Erdman's introductions. However, their work and the intentions behind its inclusion are often left for students and the audience to draw their own conclusions and make connections.

Whether this might be perceived as the antithesis of curation and/or an experiment in collective curation, it is nonetheless an impressive roster of artists and an indubitable collection of stunning

work. With a range of more or less established artists whose praxes oscillate from visual arts, industrial design, land art, culinary art, and just dead on intermedia the content on the following pages expands (beyond expectation) our understanding of "architectural" contexts and mediums into a broader field of intellectual discourse. Mediums ranging from photography, colossal textiles, dirt, thick viscous fluids, drawing, and cinema, each contribution allows us to draw upon not only the mediums sessions in a more focused manner, but also widen our understanding of each designer or thinker's understanding of the term.

Similarly, the manners by which artist document, replicate, falsify, mirror or reflect contexts, be it of a gallery, courtyard or landscape their work enriches and deepens the prospect of new ways to conceive of context. The following pages could perhaps be seen as a visual epilogue, a meditation on the palindromic bookends (Mediums and Contexts), on the center-piece introductions and essays, allowing one to interlace the ideas captured throughout the book and enticing one to project and explore them further.

Images of Pop-Up Exhibitions and receptions following Pratt Sessions

Rafael Lozano Hemmer, *Vectorial Elevation, Zócalo Square, Mexico City*
1999

(Artist selected by Eric Höweler)

Gregory Crewdson, *Untitled*

2004

(Artist selected by Marcelo Spina)

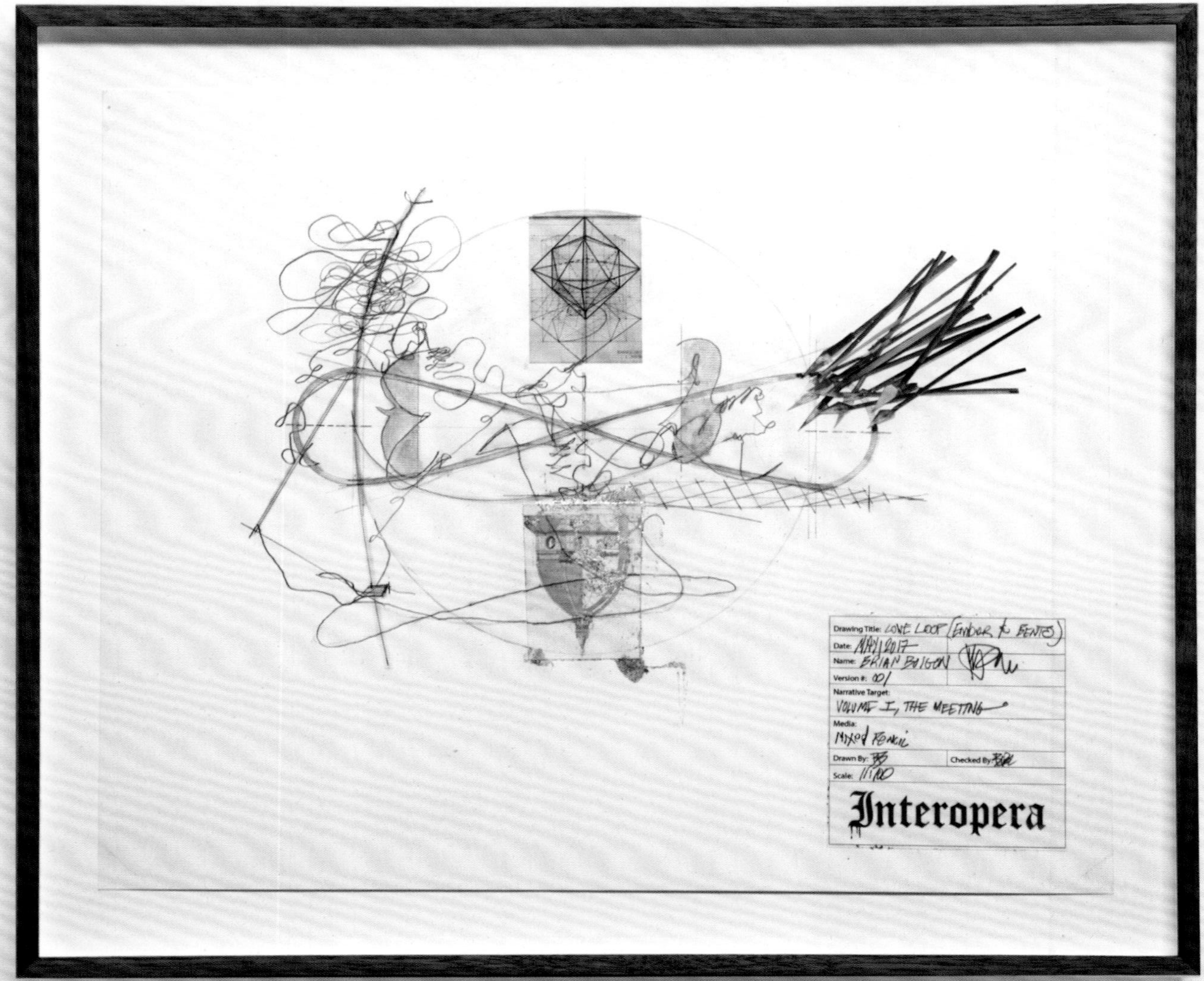


Brian Boigon, *LOVE LOOP*
Mixed media: pencil, metal leaf and collage on paper

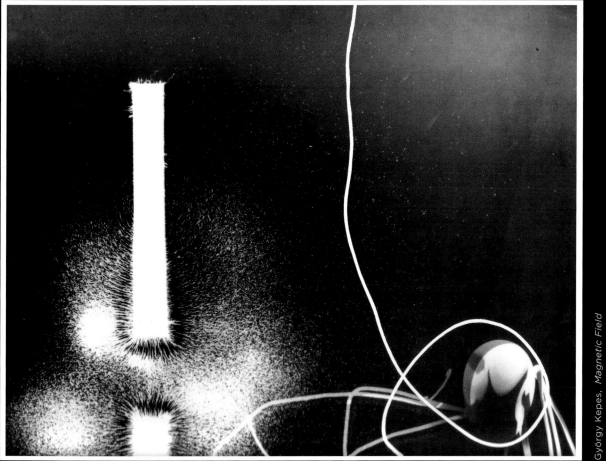

György Kepes, *Magnetic Field*
ca. 1938
(Artist selected by Bruce Mau)

# a r
# + d
## APPLIED
## RESEARCH
## +DESIGN
## PUBLISHING

Published by Applied Research and Design Publishing, an imprint of ORO Editions.

Gordon Goff: Publisher

www.appliedresearchanddesign.com
info@appliedresearchanddesign.com

Graphic Design: Jeff Anderson
Editor: Original Copy
AR+D Project Coordinator: Kirby Anderson

10  9  8  7  6  5  4  3  2  1 First Edition

Library of Congress data available upon request. World Rights:
Available

ISBN: 978-1-940743-83-7

Color Separations and Printing: ORO Group Ltd.
Printed in China.

International Distribution: www.appliedresearchanddesign.com/
distribution

# Acknowledgments

**DAVID ERDMAN
CHAIRPERSON, ASSOCIATE PROFESSOR
GRADUATE ARCHITECTURE + URBAN DESIGN**

This book would not have been possible without the generous time and support of each participant in the Pratt Sessions. Their willingness to engage in a non-standard, conversation-based format, to make the extra effort to custom build presentations and to open themselves up to unpredictable subjects and discussions are all reconfirmations of their station as leaders and their insatiable curiosity as thinkers. Their counterpart artist nominees for the Pop-Up Exhibitions deserve special thanks as well, for their willingness to share their work in relation to these sessions with the students and faculty of the GAUD, School of Architecture, and Institute at large. I would like to especially thank the Dean Tom Hanrahan for his willing support on this project and for extending the latitude to enrich the public programs and printed discourse of the School of Architecture with specific respect to the GAUD. I would like to equally thank Kirk Pillow, Provost, whose comprehensive support of this project has enabled us to galvanize our interests and capacities as a department and faculty within the local, national, and international design and arts communities.

Without student interest none of this would be possible and I would like to specifically thank the Graduate Student Council members for their support and participation in these events. I would also like to thank all faculty who have attended these events, asked questions, participated in and/or contributed to this book, not only for their efforts but also for exploring these subjects unfettered and allowing us the collaborative space to test and debate them in an exceptional and rare showing of collegiality and collective will.

Behind the book and each of the events is an impeccable team of colleagues who have been the pillars upon which all of this possible. Our editor Julia van den Hout and her team at Original Copy, as well as Jeff Anderson, the GAUD Special Projects Coordinator, have been unwavering in their efforts and commitment to this project, finessing all the errors and collaborating to curate and shape the content in the most meaningful ways. We are very thankful for Gordon Goff, Kirby Anderson, and Jake Anderson of Oro for their support and their assistance with this publication. Special thanks go out to the current and former Assistant Chairs (Alex Barker and Phil Parker, respectively) whose input, insights, and collaboration have been invaluable throughout the sessions. Erin Murphy, Gloria Nyaega, and Geoff Olsen, who run and oversee the operations of the GAUD office and the IT staff, all help in different ways to prepare and manage each event and insure that all participants are warmly welcomed to the GAUD, and that all goes smoothly. Last but not least, we thank the many student Graduate Assistants over the past year—Jacob Myers, Haya Alnibari, Yomna Dabat, Jeffrey Gaudet, and Nai Hua Chen have been the engine behind the preparation and research for each these events and this book.

Finally, my wife Karvina deserves my dearest and loving thanks for tolerating the late evenings into which these events inevitably extended, the long hours of pre-event preparation, and the considerable distraction that resulted from taking this project under my wing among my many parallel and competing duties as Chair and as husband; all while she was pregnant.

# Image Credits, Mediums

# Image Credits, Contexts

| | |
|---|---|
| 8 | Stanley Saitowitz/Natoma Architects Inc. |
| 9 | Alexander Severin |
| 10 | 1. Richard Barnes / 2. Bruce Damonte / 3. Stanley Saitowitz/ Natoma Architects Inc. / 4. Bruce Damonte / 5. Stanley Saitowitz/Natoma Architects Inc. / 6. Bruce Damonte / 7–9. Richard Barnes |
| 11 | 10. Michael Moran / 11. Paul Warchol / 12. Henry Smith-Miller / 13. Alexander Severin / 14. Michael Moran / 15. Brad Feinknopf-OTTO / 16. Henry Smith-Miller |
| 14 | Stanley Saitowitz/Natoma Architects Inc. |
| 15 | [top] Bruce Damonte; [bottom] Stanley Saitowitz/Natoma Architects Inc. |
| 16 | Tim Griffith, courtesy Stanley Saitowitz/Natoma Architects Inc. |
| 17 | Bruce Damonte |
| 18 | Richard Barnes |
| 19 | Bruce Damonte |
| 20 | [top] Jock Pottle; [bottom] Paul Warchol |
| 21 | [top] Brad Feinknopf/OTTO, [middl; [bottom] Michael Moran |
| 22 | Michael Moran |
| 23 | Paul Warchol |
| 24 | Michael Moran |
| 25 | Brad Feinknopf/OTTO |
| 27 | Courtesy of Pratt Institute, GAUD |
| 28 | [top] Tim Griffith, courtesy Stanley Saitowitz/Natoma Architects Inc.; [bottom] Bruce Damonte |
| 29 | Michael Moran |
| 30 | Roland Halbe |
| 31 | Rural Urban Framework |
| 32 | All images Ensamble Studio |
| 33 | All images Rural Urban Framework |
| 36 | Roland Halbe |
| 37 | [top] Iwan Baan; [bottom] Roland Halbe |
| 38 | Ensamble Studio |
| 39 | Roland Halbe |
| 40 | Ensamble Studio |
| 41 | Roland Halbe |
| 43–47 | Rural Urban Framework |
| 49 | Courtesy Pratt Institute, GAUD |
| 50 | Iwan Baan |
| 51 | Morphosis Architects |
| 52 | 1. Steven Holl / 2. Michael Moran / 3. Steven Holl Architects / 4. Paul Warchol / 9–10. Paul Warchol / 11. Shu He / 14. Iwan Baan |
| 53 | 5. Thom Mayne with Mike Nesbit and El Nopal Press, Morphosis 6. Morphosis Architects / 7. Iwan Baan / 8, 12. Morphosis / 13. Vincent Desjardins / 15. Morphosis |
| 56 | Suk Lee |
| 57–58 | Iwan Baan |
| 59 | Paul Warchol |
| 60 | Suk Lee |
| 61 | Paul Warchol |
| 62 | Morphosis Architects |
| 63 | [top] Nic Lehoux; [bottom] Beyond My Ken |
| 64 | Morphosis Architects |
| 65 | Iwan Baan |
| 66 | Morphosis Architects |
| 67 | Iwan Baan |
| 69 | Courtesy Pratt Institute, GAUD |

# Image Credits, Overview

| | |
|---|---|
| M09 | Monica Nouwens |
| M10 | Courtesy of Höweler + Yoon |
| M11 | David Gillespie |
| M12 | Courtesy of Sanford Kwinter |
| M13 | Courtesy of Leeser Architecture |
| M14 | Courtesy of Neil M. Denari Architects |
| M15 | Courtesy of Santiago Piedrafita |
| M18 | Courtesy of Pratt Institute, GAUD |
| M19 | Rafael Lozano Hemmer |
| M20 | Gregory Crewdson. Courtesy Gagosian |
| M21 | Brian Boigon, image courtesy of Christie Contemporary, photo by Adam Swica |
| M22 | Estate of György Kepes: Juliet Kepes Stone & Imre Kepes |
| M23 | Jeffrey Milstein |
| M24 | Marco Brambilla |

| | |
|---|---|
| C10 | Courtesy of Stanley Saitowitz |
| C11 | Courtesy of Laurie Hawkinson |
| C12 | Courtesy of Ensamble Studio |
| C13 | Courtesy of Rural Urban Framework |
| C14 | Courtesy of Steven Holl Architects |
| C15 | Courtesy of Morphosis Architects |
| C16 | Courtesy of Pratt Institute, GAUD |
| C18 | Araceli Paz, courtesy of PUJOL |
| C19 | 2018 Robert Irwin / Artists Rights Society (ARS), New York |
| C20 | 1969 Christo |
| C21 | Thomas Demand, VG Bild-Kunst, Bonn / SIAE, Rome |
| C22 | Sarah Oppenheimer |
| C23 | Matthew Ritchie |

Matthew Ritchie, *The Morning Line*
2008
(Artist selected by Thom Mayne)

Sarah Oppenheimer, *D-33*
2012
(Artist selected by Steven Holl)

MEDIUMS

CONTEXTS

Vol. 1

CONTEXTS

# Pratt Sessions

# Contexts

# David Erdman
# New Architectural Contexts

One half of the Pratt Sessions focuses on New Architectural Contexts. The intention of focusing on this subject is to sharpen "context" within our own terms as a set of graduate programs on the east coast. We see context as a vague, sloppy, and ill-defined term that continues to be propped up as the holy grail of architectural authenticity, communal value, and appropriateness, and yet is limited in its usage; theoretical and/ or practical examinations. For us, context nicely encapsulates an array of contemporary debates ranging from the socio-political inequities of development to environmental responsiveness and is here, through the Pratt Sessions, placed on the chopping block as a means to principally investigate whether or not these two aspects of contexts *are* really the kingpins of twenty-first century urban, suburban, and rural contexts or simply just decoys and marketing terms used to prop up otherwise mediocre buildings and site strategies.

The aim of these three sessions is to examine the eccentricities of the twenty-first century city at large—its density, its experiential qualities, and its design opportunities—through the lens of various established and emerging designers' and thinkers' work in New York City, Los Angeles, and other west coast and asian cities. This focus is an intentional shift from understanding the city as a language, a pattern and, quantitative data toward an understanding that is indiscernibly about urbanity and its "live" qualities. Each of the Pratt Sessions participants offers a vantage point on the subject of architectural contexts, and each pairing raises specific questions surrounding the prospect of those subjects: namely what is an "architectural" context and why would our renewed understanding of it be valuable now or in the future?

From invigorated understandings of the thick, compact edge to explorations of void-objects, from primal prefabrication to entropic community-based architectures, and from capillary urbanism to the notion of an urban palimpsest, the designers and thinkers comprising these three Pratt Sessions suggest a turn in our understanding of context. Each firm is accomplished if not lauded for its range of projects and approach to design. Underscoring those works are writings and texts introspecting their variegated methods of fabrication, design, and praxes,

which further uproot our typical understandings of how architecture relates to its surroundings.

Collectively the three sessions flip some of the conventional notions of context upside down. The participants' works stand as cases of best practices for how architecture generates contexts as opposed to merely responding to them. While working closely with the existing assets of the contexts in which their projects are sited—in some cases the literal materials and labor from the site—their work also explicitly projects, transforming and displacing the origins of that context synthetically and aggressively; the work is neither passive nor polite. The way each designer enmeshes context into architecture is an active and live set of processes and qualities; excavating, suspending, permeating, compacting or bending. The array of projects across three sessions make clear the composite practices required to engage a contemporary context. Landscape, urban design, conservation, and architecture are all deployed in tandem requiring a quiver of tools and an imagination to bring those disparate and unrelated ecologies together into one design.

The sessions skirt and directly affront a disciplinary etymology of the word "context," which is complex and multifaceted. This meandering and range from the oblique to the head on is intentional. We use the term context to perturb and agitate our participants, their work, and our attendant audiences into a conversation about what is otherwise a sensitive subject. To set up the discussion we have accounted for what we understand to be two mainstream disciplinary benchmarks that are common hallmarks of undergraduate and graduate curricula (Pratt's included).

The first benchmark is one that situates context in its semiological capacities. The diligent contextualist in this scenario is one whose project appears like and has a logical slash meaningful relationship with its surroundings. At best, context in this instantiation signifies the past and its origins while having the potential to inflect or distort both in some manner. Techniques of collage or encapsulating specific geographic typologies in the form of regionalist vernaculars and materialities anchor this benchmark. Think Colin Rowe,

Aldo Rossi, and Kenneth Frampton. Or in a more contemporary context, consider Shigeru Ban, Wang Shu, and Peter Zumthor. These are all architects whose discourse is perhaps the closest thing we have to a slow food movement in architecture. It embodies work that has a strong communal innuendo if nothing else. Their work represents the "new authentic."

The second arm, and an outcome of the digital turn in the late twentieth century, is one that sees context as environment of data; often misconstrued as an "ecology," which can be mapped. The metrics of solar orientation, rising tides, diminishing cooling loads, socio-economic and political data are among other quantitative factors that may drive the design; data stands in as an alibi legitimating a form-finding logic. This results in a design by inevitability. "I'm a designer, I want to harness the context, I map all the forces, and that results in a building." Think parametric in whatever form it may rear its head.

On behalf of our students, their curiosity, and their future, we are not okay with this being it: with these two approaches/ methods being the limit of ideas for a definitive architectural context. How do we account for buildings that do not appear anything like their surroundings and, while being environmentally responsible, do not necessarily flaunt those parameters as their formal alibi? Perhaps even more important is the subject of origin, authenticity, and ontology. Does the site always come first and the architecture second?

*New Architectural Contexts* is thus an area of research in the GAUD and the Pratt Sessions that explores the ways in which architecture activates context; something we understand as an explicit symptom of twenty-first century cities as they become increasingly more dense and as they grow inward and accumulate on top of themselves to conserve resources— cultural, economical, and ecological. Shifting the discourse on "architecture and the city" away from the semiological and away from quantitative performance-based design, the focus in the sessions is understanding architectural context as that which is fundamentally premised on the design of urban qualities.

The reformulation of architectural praxes that results from this re-centering of context in the discipline is of equal interest and a center point of each of the practices encapsulated in these conversations and sessions. No longer the last step of municipal planning, this strain of investigation examines how architecture is situated as the "early prototype," re-postulating codes and probing the potentials of a rapidly densifying city and/or its vacuous rural complement. Demanding the intertwining of architecture, landscape architecture, urban design, interior design, and conservation, and operating at a scale larger than a building yet smaller than the city, these designers push to an extreme concepts of architectural alteration and re-origination, challenging conventional notions of adaptive re-use, infill, development, authenticity, and conservation.

"New" is thus not intended as a descriptor for the unfounded or exotic geographies yet to be colonized by progressive design and/or technology nor a search for an essentialistic regionally-based authentic. It is not necessarily even concerned with what is next. "New" is instead what is right in front of our eyes. In the framework of these sessions it is a blunt admission that the cities we operate in no longer fit the morphological patterns of the prior century, nor that our resultant disciplinary apparatus is well-formed for engaging the contemporary or future city. New thinking, new understanding, new approaches that alter and allow us to recapitulate existing cites, existing villages and existing sites is the *new* we are seeking; post-digital turn, with a fresh eye toward the multitude of media and praxes we can now tinker with, from low tech to high tech, from cost effective to cutting edge. This is the focus of these sessions and what we believe to be a pertinent discussion to the future city and profession.

Stanley
Saitowitz

# Introduction

## DAVID ERDMAN

This evening's session is devoted to the subject of New Architectural Contexts and whether our understanding of the word "context" continues to be valuable. Stanley Saitowitz and Laurie Hawkinson are the exemplars par excellence of a **rare and hybrid architect**, who thirsts not to settle, who continues to learn, and is ultimately willing to engage, discuss, and unpack issues that may deepen or thwart our own disciplinary insecurities and expectations.

In 1993, they were featured along with seven other architects in a film, directed by Michael Blackwood, that largely drew upon emerging East and West Coast talents, deeming them as the "new modernists." These architects all incited the disciplinary influences on their work as an equal if not more important aspects than the regional influences of the sites on which their projects were located. These architects are building on the principles of modernism, while evolving a new language drawn from politics, film, literature, theory, and the state of the world. The movie encapsulates one of the first things that I believe all designers must consider: the **duality if not multiplicity of the contexts** in which we work. At a minimum, we can refer to context as one's disciplinary method versus contexts as a series of test cases and/or specific "sites" for ongoing research.

As the movie implies, we could talk about the similarities present between Laurie and Stanley's work, and/or about a shared sensibility that embraces the use of "raw" products. However, I would like to take this opportunity to instead establish some distinguishing characteristics between their work that may give insight as to the possibilities of **the term context within the discipline**.

I am a fan of both firms' work because their projects don't look anything like their surroundings. Yet, I would not say that either designer or firm is engaged in a project of **contextual or disciplinary "autonomy."** To the contrary, I believe there is a more sophisticated game at play here; one that **relies on semi-autonomy** as a contextual device and a tactic that one could speculate will be of increasing importance in the future development of dense cities. As much as this **contextual effect** may be a **consciously or unconsciously shared desire**, the approach toward producing it is markedly different.

Stanley's work is undeniably volumetric, **01** rhythmic, **02** and compact. **03** He is among few designers who adroitly navigates one of the primary challenges facing our cities today:

densification. Working with simple rectangular forms that give an initial monolithic impression, **04** Stanley's projects are not often what they appear to be from a distance. Solids are rhythmically complemented with meandering **complex interior void figures 05** that meander in section, **06** adorned with lush textures, **07** his work has a **sophisticated and unmistakable porosity** and **ephemerality**. **08** The voids **reverse conventional disciplinary assumptions**. They are less subtractions than they are devices that interiorize the exterior; taking on object-like qualities.

While immaculately executed, detailed, and studied with the utmost skill, his prefabricated modular constructions are not legible as discrete modular parts, nor are his green roofs a cartoonish veneer. Instead they reinforce this interplay between **the volume** and **the ephemeral**, **the smooth** and **the rough 09** in ways that allow seemingly uninhabitable and intensely dense spaces to have a rich, almost **magical lightness** that makes them both **desirable and inhabitable**.

Laurie's work, with her firm Smith-Miller + Hawkinson is **on the "edge." 10** Playing with "boundaries" between land and water, inside and outside, **11** or two nations, **12** there seems to be a concerted effort to **work, re-work, fold, and transform edge**—thickening it and imbuing it with "mediatric" qualities. Often deploying super-graphics that give an otherwise thin space depth, or, what I would like to suggest, tinker with the space between a **Venturian thinness** and **Eisenmanian depth**. The cinematic effect of the work imbues a sense of simultaneous explosion and compaction. The sheen of glass and metal in oblique orientations **13** further intensify and animate the trajectories and lines of their work. **14** As edges become more variegated, be it a result of rising tides of a pier and/or socio-political complexities of a border crossing, the work seems to be one that **enmeshes context 15** into what is often seen as **not a space at all** but an edge. **16**

Whether it is through the vibration of **compact volumetrics** or the **cinematic mediation of an edge**, the projects conceived by both Stanley and Laurie do not fit in; at least in the ways one might expect a building to fit into its context—by looking like its neighbors. Instead, their projects **agitate** and perhaps even go so far as to reconstruct those contexts often calling into question which came first. Their buildings are at once **tethered and engrained** into their sites as much as they are **tenuous and alien**. It is for these reasons that their thoughts and insights are relevant to the Pratt Sessions and the inaugural launch of the series and first foray into this subject; New Architectural Contexts.

# Stanley Saitowitz

## SAN FRANCISCO, CA

I'm going to show projects through the lens of two contexts. One is related to place and the other is related to time. The context of place involves the actual bounded site; the figure. It surrounds both immediate and distant; the ground. Figure/ground are mutually interdependent, shifting attention from object to relation in an overlapping coexistence where part is always comingled with whole.

The context of time involves presentness and the general conditions of contemporary culture—the ideological landscape and attitudes of our times, the states of technology and environment, what architecture is now as an accumulated presence of all its history. This present is what differentiates the existing ground and the new figure. Each building aims to be connected, but also to mark its moment.

Architecture's central project is the building of the city. Each contributing part must be more than itself; charging the spaces around, making connections, adding to the whole. Urban buildings, which participate in this tradition, are antidotes to the extravagant expressionism of so much current signature architecture. Rather than originality, they focus on collective form. Rather than plastic configurations of fantasy, the goal is the continuity of the city.

The urban environment is not a series of independent objects fighting in a field, but a historic process of evolution and development.

In San Francisco, there are 197,000 building parcels or sites. Of those, 173,000 or 87.8 percent are residential. Housing is by far the most important constituent element of the fabric of the city, the prime ingredient of its urban grain. San Francisco used to be made up of a variety of distinct neighborhood architectures, which led to a rich urban fabric.

Our work is a search to reinvigorate the unique characteristics of each side. Our three new Victorians on Natoma Street have been a laboratory for our urban buildings; our office at number 1022, number 1028 next door, and number 1029 across the street.

Where the 101 Freeway ends, 8 Octavia is a gateway building, announcing the new San Francisco. Victorian ornament becomes modern instrument, more like an iPhone than a corset, with operable fins that enable occupants to modulate light and sound.

At California College of the Arts, we converted the 1950s SOM Walter Netsch Greyhound Bus Service building, inspired by IIT, to be the language for new freshman dorms and build an identity for the campus.

Stanley Saitowitz / Natoma Architects, 1022 and 1028 Natoma Street, San Francisco, CA, 2005

Stanley Saitowitz / Natoma Architects, Hubbel Street, San Francisco, CA

Stanley Saitowitz / Natoma Architects, 8 Octavia,
San Francisco, CA, 2014

On Vine Street in Los Angeles, where large commercial boulevards contrast with residential streets, our building steps from the scale of a tower down to the scale of the neighborhood. Staggered balconies project into the sunlight. Six historical bungalows are preserved and are connected by a new alleyway.

Each project involves conversations with the found conditions of the context of place and time. Each infecting and inflecting the other through continuity, where consistent addition is woven with the whole. Abstraction, where general rules and concepts are extracted from found conditions. Condensation, where image, memory, and thought merge to create a displacement and something new. Densification, where concentration intensifies. Measure, where reference and reflection provide dimension. And translation, where meaning is communicated through equivalency.

Stanley Saitowitz / Natoma Architects, Vine Street, Los Angeles, CA

Stanley Saitowitz and Laurie Hawkinson

Stanley Saitowitz / Natoma Architects, Yerba Buena Lofts,
San Francisco, CA, 2001

Stanley Saitowitz / Natoma Architects, OZ Residence,
Atherton, CA, 2017

Stanley Saitowitz / Natoma Architects, Center for Jewish Life, Drexel University, Philadelphia, PA, 2016

Stanley Saitowitz / Natoma Architects, OZ Residence,
Atherton, CA, 2017

# Laurie Hawkinson

**NEW YORK, NY**

David has asked Stanley and me to go down the slippery slope of using our work—built or otherwise—to address the term "context" in architecture. All the complexity of an architectural project, especially a built project, makes it difficult to stand as evidence. To discuss new actionable understandings of the term in relation to architecture in urban and rural areas, I will first go back to how we might be interpreting this term.

In the earliest uses, *context* meant, "the weaving together of the words in language." This sense, now obsolete, developed logically from the word's source in Latin, *contexere*, as in, "to weave or join together." By current definitions, *context* considers "the surroundings, circumstances, environment, background, or settings that determine, specify, or clarify the meaning of an event or other occurrence."

My exploration of this slippery slope will be constructed of a select series of projects which span the length of our practice. In thinking about this, the first question that came up is, could complete separation from the immediate context be an actionable context? What about a focus on something in the distance? Or on the spaces around the perimeter of a house, which consider the perimeter as a space of indeterminacy rather than a weather seal, especially in an urban condition like New York?

In our project for the Museum of Women's History in New York, which was done in collaboration with Catherine Ingraham, a driver is the space within the building that the Statue of Liberty would see if she looked over her left shoulder. Part of the idea was to ask, "what would she see of us and what would we see of her?"

A second consideration was the section through that condition, which developed a void space in the building. It was a consideration of the skin of the building relative to the Battery Park City neighborhood's covenant restriction, which requires the window-to-wall ratio to be between 30 and 50 percent. We went to the lowest ratio to produce a screen for a double wall museum in which the inner layer of a thermos-like space has a higher level of control.

Considering context in our projects brings up several more questions.

Smith-Miller + Hawkinson Architects, Museum of Women's History, The Leadership Center, New York, 2002

Smith-Miller + Hawkinson Architects with Barbara Kruger, North Carolina Museum of Art Masterplan and Amphitheater, Raleigh, NC, 1997

**20**

Smith-Miller + Hawkinson Architects, OSU Wilce Student Health Center,
Columbus, OH, 2015

Can a material be both the subject or program for the
building and a major part of its physical assembly? Can text be
considered context for program?

Can the driver of a net zero resiliency plan in an 80-acre site
be considered context for a larger rural relationship?

Can a material and its fabrication and assembly process
provide context?

Can a border between two countries be actionable?
Understanding a border not as a line you cross from one
country to the other, but as perpendicular. Our Land Port of
Entry in Champlain, NY, located on the border of the United
States and Canada, faces north, so it's always in shade.

Can a canopy create an edge that creates a space?

Can infrastructure, in the basic physical and organizational
sense of the structure needed for the operation of a society or
an enterprise, be considered an actionable understanding of
context, as in our Zerega Avenue EMS Station in the Bronx?

And can a green roof be considered context, not just as an
additional sustainable piece, but as a component in context?

This brings me back to my initial question of whether this
slippery slope, in which one asserts that a relatively small first
step leads to a chain of related events culminating in some
effect, depends on the warrant of whether or not one can
demonstrate a process that leads to a significant event.

It ignores the possibility of middle ground and assumes a
discrete transition from category A to category B. A middle
ground possibility is acknowledged and reasoning is provided
for the likelihood of the predicted outcome, which is what I've
attempted to do here.

Smith-Miller + Hawkinson Architects, United States Land Port of Entry,
Massena, NY, 2009

Smith-Miller + Hawkinson Architects, Zerega Avenue EMS Station #3,
Bronx, NY, 2013

Stanley Saitowitz and Laurie Hawkinson

Smith-Miller + Hawkinson Architects, United States Land Port of Entry,
Massena, NY, 2009

Smith-Miller + Hawkinson Architects with Barbara Kruger, North Carolina
Outdoor Cinema and Amphitheater, Raleigh, NC, 1997

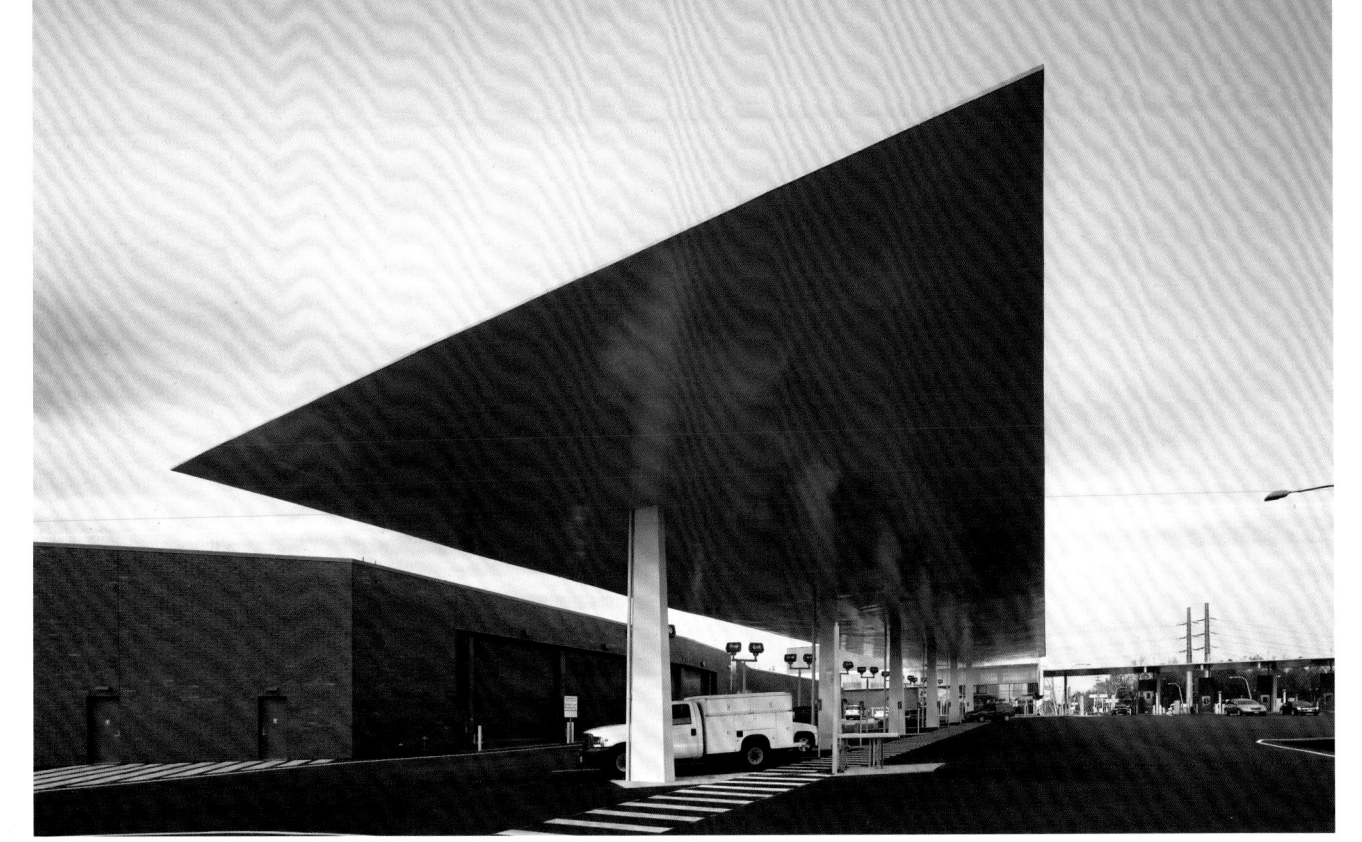

Smith-Miller + Hawkinson Architects, United States Land Port of Entry,
Massena, NY, 2009

Smith-Miller + Hawkinson Architects, OSU Wilce Student Health Center,
Columbus, OH, 2015

# Conversation

## STANLEY SAITOWITZ AND LAURIE HAWKINSON

**David Erdman (DE):** Thank you for your presentations and taking on the challenge of having to address a large topic. Laurie, you focused on the actionable as an idea about context, and Stanley, you brought up both place and time. Both of those seem to have a temporal component to them.

As much as we can look at the existing found condition, the inevitable problem with architecture is that we're being asked to design in places that are unstable, *and* we are asked to design something for the future in a context that isn't yet there. In graduate programs and architecture schools more broadly, I feel there's a disciplinary assumption that if we map a context accurately enough, we could make an appropriate response. Both of your work is very thoughtful and sensitive to some of those existing conditions, but I also see a consistency of methods and ideas that are being brought to a site and that also actively change it. There seems to be a willingness to acknowledge unstable environments. How conscious is that and do you agree that it can be a productive way of operating?

**Stanley Saitowitz (SS):** The complexity of working in a city like San Francisco, which has a planning department that is an authoritarian entity that demands context and has the power to force you to do buildings in a certain way, is what has motivated my work. I don't try to be naughty, but you can't help it. San Francisco is such a precious, pretty place that you do want to kick it around a bit.

**DE:** I was just going to ask about your relationship with the code—I have always seen your reading of the San Francisco code as at once incredibly adroit and a very close read of what is there, but largely to subvert it. For example, you were one of the first people to do away with the bay window by perversely using precisely the code that was used to maintain traditional bay windows and constrain the language of designers. Laurie, you brought up a similar consideration with your mention of the Museum of Women's History.

**Laurie Hawkinson (LH):** When you're working within constraints, which also provide the context, you often tell a story about the project to get it by, whatever that might be. It can become a whole parallel argument to what you're trying to do. Not to tell war stories, but for another project we did with the federal government, a port of entry at the Canadian border, our client was both Homeland Security and the people that are in charge of the port. I thought erroneously enough that somehow this would be like a visitor's center; that people would want to come into this building and that it should be light-filled. But, in fact, if you go in there, you're in big trouble.

As an architect, you're working to create a quality, or improve the quality of life in places like this for people who would just as soon be in a concrete box because they'd feel secure. At the same time, you're trying to find new ways of working or proposing new materials that they're not familiar with, and ways of assembling or presenting them so that they are still comfortable. In some of these cases, you're able to get a lot of architecture done on the side because there's a decoy involved. I think it's fun.

**DE:** Part of that recognizes the duplicity of the role of the architect and that there's an internal "project" that you're working on, whether it's those codes or the security demands of a client. That *misbehavior* is, to some extent, your free will and an interest to further certain practices that are internal to your firm. Those are disciplinary methods that you've been working on over many years, and there's a desire to see that evolve and grow. While there also seems to be a desire for some consistency across them, which some might see as being unsympathetic to context.

**SS:** The clients that I work for are mostly developers, and they are probably as difficult as any client you can get. The only way that you can get slack with them is when you get the numbers right. If you get your efficiency to be 85 percent, they don't bother you about how you deal with architectural questions. I think there's always that play between the story and the real story.

**DE:** To what extent do you have an interest in making your buildings more present than their surroundings or using your buildings to possibly resituate an otherwise legible historical narrative? Are you interested in sustaining the narrative or do you have an interest in situating your building as something that might've come before the other ones that were there historically?

**SS:** Now, with Google Earth, I've stopped going on site visits. I am usually so disappointed when I go and see the real place. I remember once hearing Antoine Predock talk about going camping to "feel the spirits." I don't really care about the existing site. The last thing I want to do is design anything that's like what's already there.

**LH:** I'm interested in producing not necessarily something I know or that's known, but something that I don't know. I'm also interested in testing new materials and new ways of putting things together. I don't want to repeat. I'm interested in somehow continuing a discussion that we're working on already

within the work. The point I was trying to make obliquely in my questions was that context could be manifested in a number of ways. It could just be a material, or it could be something as broad as a huge ecosystem. Context and complexity is not necessarily a surface material.

**DE:** I think that's a nice segue to open it up to students or faculty.

**Adam Chernick:** One problem I always find is navigating subjectivity. What are your processes to create a productive connection to your context, when there are so many different processes to create this connection? What are some of the signs that this connection is productive instead of reductive?

**SS:** I'm less interested in the idea of subjectivity in art and more interested in something like cooking and ingredients—putting them together in ways that taste good. I don't think what we do is that subjective. It's a process. When you're going to make a meal, you go to the grocery store, you see what looks good, you collect it, take it home, and you use recipe books. I think that's a better model for what architecture does than the "it's art" mentality and the idea that it comes out of dreams. I go to work every day. I'm there at 8:30am. I sit at my desk and I work until I get excited about something that I'm doing. I'm more focused on the idea that we are assembling things that are in the world.

**LH:** I'm also not on the subjectivity side. Architecture is very collaborative. You're always working with several people. I always call it the "$10,000 meeting" when all the consultants are around the table. You're talking with the engineers and trying to figure out these problems that you've set up for yourself. It's difficult to say what "context" is because a building is so complex.

**Thom Mayne (TM):** It seems your work is quite different

from each other and part of it is perhaps related to time. Your part-to-whole relationship reveals that the two of you are quite opposite.

Laurie, I would say your part-to-whole is relaxed. There's a slippage of elements. Your interest with graphic quality—that its surface effect is diminishing the architecture in terms of materiality—is establishing a different relationship to time. You sense architecture's ephemerality. It seems like there's a constant erosion of the work into two-dimensional stuff.

Stanley, it seems like you're quite opposite at that level. Your work is more platonic, just about Miesian in some cases. It seems to be looking for perfection, and with that, some notion of timelessness, in the most classical architectural sense. When you have your work photographed, it's always based on your idealized state of perfection. You can't—like Mies—put the funky light shade or a funny drape somewhere. It demands an accommodation to your vision of architecture.

**SS:** There's an element of Mies that I'm completely interested in, which is the dematerializing of the object, the removal of connection, the almost seamlessness of the actual making of a thing. But in terms of the actual object's life, I'm interested in it as being an apparatus, almost like an instrument that's dedicated to the freedom of the people who occupy it. By taking out all the overlay of formality and creating this sort of neutrality, I see it as "opening it up" for others to occupy. I would say that 80 percent of what I do is for unknown clients. I build houses for people who are generic beings and that I know have two legs, two arms, eyes, and a nose. I know nothing about the occupants in detail. What I try to give them is an apparatus for them to explore—like a canvas. So, while you might be reading it as perfection, for me, it's about emptiness. It's about the de-objectification.

**TM:** It has become so rigorous. Your OZ Residence was incredibly precise. There was absolutely no interest in any description of structure. It's a pure cantilever as it touches the surface. I'm thinking of the inside, which I don't think you showed. It reminds me of Craig Ellwood, who was my teacher; we were walking through his Rosen House and just by instinct, he walked around the house, moving and making symmetrical all the pieces. And it was absolutely demanding because the house was so pure.

**SS:** I'm exactly the opposite. I have a penthouse in a building that I built and there are eighteen units. The biggest pleasure for me is to visit other people in the building and see how they've occupied the same space as what I have. One has a red wall. One has antiques. When I show the interiors of my buildings, that's one of the things that I try to demonstrate; I'm creating a frame and I want somebody else to make the picture. That

David Erdman (left), Laurie Hawkinson (center), and Stanley Saitowitz (right) in conversation at Pratt Sessions 01

Natoma Architects, 1028 Natoma Street, San Francisco, CA, 2005

house was photographed before it was inhabited.

**TM:** Do you agree with my essence of you? You're deconstructing the solidity with a clear idea of graphic and the letter forms become part of that.

**SS:** I would disagree with the use of classicist as a label. It has a refinement. It is about a certain kind of elimination of objecthood. I work in my office that I built maybe thirty years ago and it has exposed chasses and everything—all the connections are articulated. And I realize that I'm no longer only interested in the Renzo Piano kind of world of explaining how things are made. I care a lot about structure and order.

**TM:** But you seem to be interested in the platonic idea like the Tendenza, Aldo Rossi, Hans Kollhoff, or Josef Paul Kleihues.

**SS:** Those are not my heroes at all. I'm interested in Kazuyo Sejima, Aires Mateus, work like that.

**Thomas Leeser:** I think this is the point when you all can get at each other's throats, which we are all begging for. You both have this incredible interest in detail. Except Stanley, you want to dispute it and Laurie, you want to show it, right?

**LH:** I'm not interested in showing how it's made. I'm interested in discussing the differences between things. The differences but not necessarily how something is made.

**DE:** It's quite interesting that when Michael Blackwood's movie came out, one of the things that I believe would've been associated with your work, twenty-something years ago, was that craft and the "joinery," etc. If you look at Laurie's The Dillon or you look at Stanley's Tampa Museum of Art, they're both very "taut." You don't see the joinery so much anymore. Both have different cinematic effects. Especially at The Dillon, the oblique really plays with sheen in ways that give it a very coarse texture as you move around it on the street and through the toroidal staircases. You can get into a discussion about how those "ephemeralities," the "cinematics," and the effects of both of your work and the geometries each of you use produce

Natoma Architects, OZ Residence, Atherton, CA, 2017

different effects. I think there could be a discussion surrounding orthogonality versus the oblique and to what extent the implicit contrast between the two fractures a project or does the opposite and gives it a cohesion and architectural holism. There may be a range of difference there through that thinking in terms of the cinematic effect being a little less cohesive.

**LH:** I would agree with Thom's assessment of the frontality. Henry [Smith-Miller] and I are certainly more interested in a kind of oblique and looking at something from the edge to reveal material, or maybe not, but to reveal something not from that frontal condition. With Stanley's work, I don't know if it's the fact that you are working in San Francisco and that tight edge, it's certainly the classicalness of that very, very hard facade. I love your description, though, of the elimination of everything from the interior, which actually horrifies me, and that you are allowing everybody to just kind of put whatever in.

**Henry Smith-Miller:** I've been sitting back here watching this discussion evolve and there is something that Laurie and I have in common with Stanley, but we didn't show it. At The Dillon, our windows pop in and out the way your louvers turn. Because we thought about the occupancy of that building modulating the skin. We were concerned with the occupation of our buildings by, as you said, "generic beings." We're all generic. But in the container there are some similarities. They're not obvious formal ones, but I think they're philosophical links.

Smith-Miller + Hawkinson Architects, The Dillon – 405 West 53rd Street Condominiums, New York, 2011

Smith-Miller + Hawkinson Architects, The Dillon – 405 West 53rd Street Condominiums, New York, 2011

Stanley Saitowitz and Laurie Hawkinson

Ensamble
Studio

# Rural Urban Framework

# Introduction

## DAVID ERDMAN

For tonight's conversation on New Architectural Contexts, we have the pleasure of welcoming four speakers: Antón García-Abril and Débora Mesa Molina from Ensamble, and Joshua Bolchover and John Lin from Rural Urban Framework (RUF). They are each emerging as a different yet significant voice on the contemporary discourse of architectural context. They're committed to practice and teaching within a somewhat unique and alternative model of that practice. Both firms are also pretty hot right now. They are snatching up an unending series of awards, are participating in a relentless list of symposia, and exhibitions, and they're part of the "circuit," riding the propulsion of their separate discourses at full speed.

Each firm engages in **aggressive yet esoteric design-build** practices. They form **community** around their work in different ways. They either work closely with the community where the project is sited or form a community of participants building the project. The materials of construction are often resourced from the physical site or nearby. Yet, while these cues may hark of responsible "localism" or "community development," these four practitioners are brought together here tonight because their work is stunning, aesthetically driven, and provocative. While one may find the work compelling because of its sensitivities to its surroundings, they do so in counter-intuitive, thoughtful, intellectually aware, and synthetic ways; they are, in my opinion, **anything but vernacular**.

I hope our discussion this evening will concentrate on the extent to which their work **re-originates the context** in ways that **do not reconstitute the aesthetics** of the existing architectures or landscapes in which they are sited.

**"New Privitivism"** or **"Extreme Brutalism"** might suffice better than any strain of authenticism one might ascribe to the work of Ensamble. Their buildings have a laissez-faire set of relationships that are somewhat between a cairn, those stacks of rocks you see on a hiking trail above the tree line, and the work of fine artist Andy Goldsworthy, whose constructions masterfully use **artifice to invoke an almost unimaginable nature**. With Ensamble, the **illusion of casual piling** 01 is underpinned by **technical mastery of balance and weight**. 02

Another aspect specific to their work is **scale**, 03 which is often warped and has a slightly Lewis Carroll-like type of effect. The size of their construction members **defamiliarizes the human subject** 04 and is seemingly implausible. Their

constructions embody a Stonehenge level of mystique. 05

A third aspect to distinguish their work is its **texture**. It is extremely **raw and rough**. 06 Rustication, a device used historically by architects to reintroduce the "hand" and to humanize otherwise overtly machined architectures (as it was the case of the Brutalist critique of modernism) is in their work gone significantly further; texture is not brutal but **psychotropic**. The roughness is often complemented by and contrasted with elements of **immense refinement and fragility**. Their work, I would suggest, is capable of capturing both the **primal effects of architecture**, and the **humane** at the same time. 07

Joshua Bolchover and John Lin of RUF, on the other hand, are fans of the **narrative capacities** of architecture. Their approach to design may be more like a Cormac McCarthy novel: you think you're reading a Western only to find that you're in the middle of a horror story. What seems familiar is turned on its head and re-appropriated in ways that **prevent stable readings**. There's a repeated **torqueing**, **bending**, and **cranking of space** in **section** and **plan**. 08 09 Their buildings often encapsulate the exterior through compact, saturated, courtyard-like formations.

**Luscious facade textures** 10 evoke a simultaneous permeability, diffuseness, and veiling of torqued forms to produce an **entropic sensibility**. The entropy in their work is incredibly **artificial**. Extraneous screens and facades veil as much as they may expose building mass. 11 Added to these illusions one discovers the use of mirroring in RUF's work; quite literally. 12 Using reflective materials to reinstate the illusion of the landscape around their projects, or grafting materials from nearby on to their projects, live mapping seems to be an active ingredient in their work, 13 where adjacencies are literally and pictorially mapped on top of and inside of their projects. This **synthetic entropy**, artificially eroding or aging the building mass, gives the work the appearance of something that might have been from that location, while at the same time having the effect of being ulterior. RUF's work looks familiar, yet has the uncanny ability to draw one into a place you never imagined and certainly not the place you intended to go. 14

In both practices, design-build and community engagement are underpinned by **evocative and intense** architectures that are as much **tethered** to their location as they are not. The work re-originates the sites in which it is located, layering on **new economies**, **new circuitry**, and **patterns of inhabitation**. Much like a chef might imaginatively use a local supply chain, I am uncertain that anyone would know or care that it's local. If it tastes good, you're on. The effects are so **vivid and engaging** in both of these practices that to some extent the **forthcoming context** in the near future of the place is more important than either its processes and/or what one presumes to be its origins.

# Ensamble Studio

## MADRID, SPAIN

**Antón Garcia Abril (AGA):** We want to start with the origins of architecture. Everything that we build comes from the Earth, and everything that we use is just mechanized and mastered by the tools, the equipment, and the technologies that we use.

**Débora Mesa Molina (DMM):** Looking at places and their transformations has always been very inspiring and revealing—whether they are pure landscapes or an urban context. Some of our work almost seems to directly emerge from its context while

Ensamble Studio, The Truffle, Costa da Morte, Spain, 2010

others are prefabricated, and can be transported and assembled almost anywhere.

**AGA:** We use the term "on site" for projects that come from the site. This is a very easy statement to make, but when it has to be transformed into a material expression, into architecture, then a complete new set of rules has to emerge. In The Truffle, our starting point came from the understanding of the site and the usage of concrete as the catalyzer, as the conglomerate that holds together all of the natural materials in the project.

**DMM:** We were trying to experiment at the domestic scale; how can architecture almost be born from the ground where it sits? In a way, we were reorganizing natural matter using the ground as formwork, using hay bales as the formwork for the interior space, and then using concrete as the material that could give strength to a mixture of soils and rocks to create a fabricated stone.

**AGA:** But what we learned with this project, and we have been practicing since, is the belonging of everything to the site. That's the cultural context, the ancestors, the references, the programmatic interpretation of what is required, matter, tools, community, resources, everything. This is what makes architecture "on site," what makes it strongly linked to a place. It's not just the usage of the trend material of that city. No, it's the integral belonging to that place.

**DMM:** In this project, we are not developing plans per se. We are allowing a lot of improvisation so that the context can play a major part. It's a process that surprised us in the end and that revealed things that were unexpected. Several years later we continued this way of thinking about architecture in Montana at the Tippet Rise Art Center. Here, we are scaling up the ideas that we explored within the domestic scale of The Truffle to the scale of a 11,000 acre Montana ranch.

**AGA:** This project started with the architectonical exercise of how to use the site as a departure point and arrive somewhere, but not bound by architecture, typologies, or history. We tried to root all our thoughts and actions in the place.

**DMM:** We were trying to forget our urban thinking, in an effort to find other systems that come from nature, like the constellations. We were experimenting with models, tests, and researching geological processes of sedimentation, erosion, fragmentation, and explosion to see what kind of spaces can emerge from these actions. In a way, we were trying to build landscapes from the landscape.

**AGA:** This has no formal agenda or interpretation through architectonic logic, other than the resources that we are using in combination with a very abstract critique process. And here, I think, the land gives us some clues about how to perform with it and the abstract work of creating those models that ultimately

Ensamble Studio, Structures of Landscape for Tippet Rise Art Center, Fishtail, MT, 2015

**DMM:** What interested us about these systems was not only that they are prefabricated, but they use very low tech materials that are available worldwide. It takes the best aspects of prefabrication, which optimizes time and construction, and makes assembly so much easier—it does not require skilled labor to fabricate very sophisticated, industrialized systems. In this case, there was no place for uncertainty. Everything needs to be perfectly pre-engineered so that everything comes together with as little conflict between the parts as possible.

**AGA:** The construction industry is focusing a lot on such systems of re-engineering buildings to be built in a pre-manufactured factory—incorporating automation, incorporating assembly logic, and trying to detach fabrication from the geographical location of the final building. We're now trying to scale this up to mid- to high-rise constructions, some of them challenging the idea of a core that is governing the center of gravity of the column of a high rise.

**DMM:** Although these projects may seem antagonistic, we are very interested in finding how to bring those logics together. We still don't have the answer, but that's the next step.

have to be given to the land to be unearthed and extracted from them.

On the other hand, if we think about an *objet trouvé*—a synthesized element of architecture, like a beam, that gives its form to its efficiency, its industriality, and prefabricability—we immediately find ourselves with a completely different set of rules. Now it all has to do with how these parts are put together; how these encounters collide, clash, and explode in a spatial response.

In the Hemeroscopium House, we transposed a technology and scale that is usually found in civil engineering on to a residential program.

**DMM:** As with The Truffle, the domestic space becomes for us the perfect laboratory to experiment. And here, the question is completely different than the questions we were asking in the previous projects. We are appropriating certain technologies and de-contextualizing them. We are using standard elements to create nonstandard architecture. But the context itself is more like recreation than a fundamental ingredient of the architecture itself. We used very heavy pre-cast concrete materials. They are produced off site, but they are coming from three hours away by truck. In the Cyclopean House, we were working on creating much lighter prefabricated elements, allowing us to make the offsite even more off site. We fabricated these pieces in Spain and transported them to the United States.

**AGA:** We were interested in getting rid of mass while maintaining all structural integrity. We did a workshop in Madrid with non-skilled workers to developed all these composites. The construction process was driven by a combination of ultra-light structures, the logic of its assembly, and the possibility of these parts to be transported lightly.

Ensamble Studio, Hemeroscopium House, Madrid, Spain, 2008

Ensamble Studio, Cyclopean House, Brookline, MA, 2015

Ensamble Studio, The Truffle, Costa da Morte, Spain, 2010

Ensamble Studio and Rural Urban Framework

Ensamble Studio, Cyclopean House, Brookline, MA, 2015

Ensamble Studio, Hemeroscopium House, Madrid, Spain, 2008

# Rural Urban Framework

## HONG KONG, CHINA

**Joshua Bolchover (JB):** The context of our work is at the frontline of the urbanization process—in the hinterlands and peripheral rural areas where the effects of urbanization are beginning to take hold. The methodology started with a journey through rural China, which allowed us to identify paradoxical and contradictory spatial, programmatic, and typological conditions. These became the drivers of our design approach. Inevitably, as the world continues to urbanize, we will witness this continued confrontation between the urban and the rural. And underlying our work is the fundamental questioning of how this uncertain territory will be defined. Through two examples, we want to discuss the impact of the urban invading the rural and its counter—the impact of the rural invading the urban.

**John Lin (JL):** While we tend to have clear images in mind of what the difference is between the urban and the rural, the two conditions collided in an age of rapid urbanization. Areas of northern China that were rural fifty years ago, today show an invasion of industrial activity. How do we work in sites that are collisions between infrastructure and landscape, between traditional and modern forms of housing? How do we engage these contradictions through design?

The first paradox that I want to talk about is this contradiction of when you build these massive infrastructures to connect remote, rural areas, you're creating massive disruptions on the ground. This happened in one of our sites—the Mulan Primary School, which was a new extension to the existing school in Mulan Village. At the back of the school, they decided to build a high-speed railway, making a massive cut in the earth. We took the funding that was provided for stabilizing the site and we added additional funding so that today the rail infrastructure is combined with an ecological infrastructure. We have a reed bed cleansing system, a toilet, and a playground.

Another paradox is that migrants go to cities in search of work, but they continue to send money back to build houses. Ironically, as more people leave these rural areas, the population goes down but the building density goes up. In our very first project, a primary school and community center in Qinmo village, which we completed in 2008-2009, we asked ourselves, what can the school as an institution provide to the village?

This school was cut right into the landscape—a rice terrace. It takes its form from a cut and fill. And today, it's the sole place in which all the members of the community, when they come back to the village once or twice a year, can gather. Right now, the village might be empty most of the time, but a few moments in the year, this growing population comes back and invades this village.

In Angdong village, we worked with an existing three-story walk up hospital on a new extension. Before, if you got sick, you would need to have a healthy relative carry you up three flights of stairs. The hospital bought a piece of land to expand. What we found was that the cost for putting in a ramp was the exact same cost as putting in an elevator. The ramp would provide access to all floors, but then we found that residents of an old people's home across the street began to use this ramp for exercise; children come here to play. Essentially, the hospital has become a place in the community for promoting health as opposed to just dealing in sickness.

**JB:** In a very different context, I'm going to talk about how the rural has been invading the urban in the case of Ulaanbaatar, Mongolia. The 1990 democratic revolution changed Mongolia from a state controlled country to a free market economy overnight. After an initial period of hardship, the discovery of raw materials, such as coal and copper, created a huge rise in the economy, and as a result, herders began to give up their herds of goats and move to the city. When the herders arrived, they simply erected their *ger*, their traditional felt tent, and they put a fence around it. In 2002, the government introduced a land law that enabled each Mongolian citizen the right to claim a 700-meter squared plot of land. Effectively, this has created a vast sprawl of what is suburbia, basic plots with gers mixed with affordable, low cost houses.

Now, over 60 percent of Ulaanbaatar's population lives in the ger districts, and over the last twenty years, the city has expanded to around thirty times its original size. We began to look at what was going on within the ger districts. We noticed that there was a type of incremental development that was occurring through each household. As they began to acquire more money, they began to make improvements to their plots. We felt that this called for a type of more agile urban strategy that could be incremental that would begin to build up over time through a series of prototypes.

We also looked at the ger itself. Its circular form is very much about the life within rather than the life outside. The ger doesn't discuss the notion of any kind of civic programs. This led us to a series of explorations, testing how we could adapt and transform it, using different techniques. We looked to create an adaptive structure that mixed the traditional or

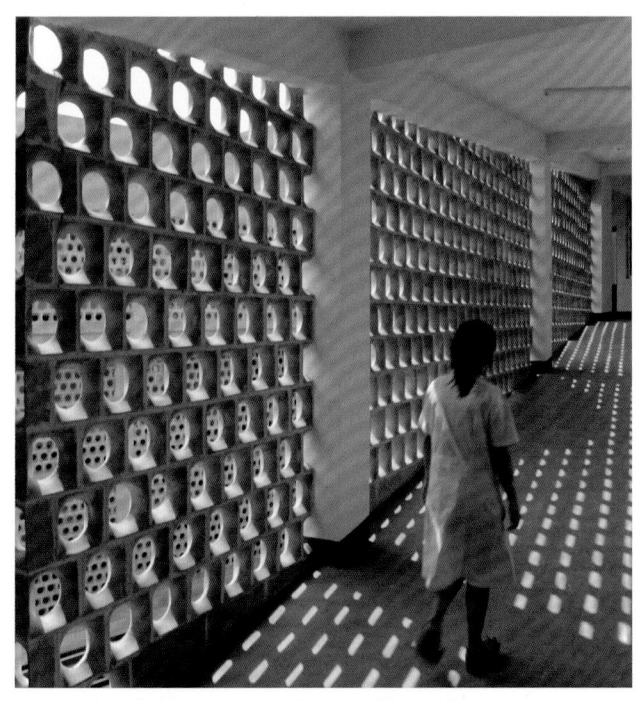

RUF, Qinmo Primary School and Community Center, Guangdong Province, China, 2008 / 2009

found structure with an insertion of a new structure—what we call the "ger plugin." Rather than rely on these large investments and complex financial mechanisms, we try to seed the infrastructure from the ger itself. And the idea is, over time, these infrastructural systems can grow within the neighborhood and begin to form a decentralized infrastructure network.

By breaking or creating a structure that begins to mediate between the fence wall and the circular structure, we're trying to transform the ger from a nomadic structure into a new type of urban typology. It offers an alternative to the low-cost brick houses which do not offer anything in terms of performance. The ger grafts itself into the building, creating a kind of hybrid living space that is part ger and part new structure. Now, given that the ger maintains a deep rooted cultural significant for Mongolians, by hybridizing the get with essential infrastructure, the ger plugin becomes an emergent new typology. Over time, the ger is not lost but becomes an active agent of Ulaanbaatar's evolution into a city that reflects its origins as a city of nomads.

RUF, Angdong Health Center, Hunan Province, China, 2014

RUF, Ger Plug-In, Ulaanbaatar, Mongolia, 2017

RUF, Ger Plug-In, Ulaanbaatar, Mongolia, 2017

RUF, Angdong Health Center, Hunan Province, China, 2014

RUF, Qinmo Primary School and Community Center, Guangdong Province,
China, 2008 / 2009

# Conversation

## DÉBORA MESA MOLINA + ANTÓN GARCÍA-ABRIL AND JOSHUA BOLCHOVER + JOHN LIN

**David Erdman (DE):** There's a very strong disciplinarian aesthetic project in both firms, as much as neither one of you tonight necessarily puts that up front. In talking about authenticity or localism, to what extent do you feel you bring it to the site and that you imbue it with a certain aesthetic that is maybe alien to the site and its origins?

**Antón García-Abril (AGA):** I think we do bring it to the site. We take a little bit, but I think we bring more than we take. If I was politically correct, I would say the contrary. But to be honest, the correct approach to a given vernacular condition or external condition is always giving rather than taking. Because if you take, you enter territory of emulation. And I think by giving, you could be even more respectful of the existing conditions and enrich the chain of tradition.

**John Lin (JL):** I don't think for us it's really a matter of obedience to the site. One of the things I appreciate about your work is this incredible aesthetic contrast between the work that you call "on site" and "off site." I often feel like a kind of architectural swindler, and it's nice to meet another master con artist, meaning this skill of being able to improvise and being able to react to the conditions of what you're faced with. With our presentation, we wanted to contrast two housing projects that are radically different, both in aesthetic and condition. One works within the context of something very traditional, like the ger. The other works against the generic, against the absence of anything traditional that is left. One is hyper-urban and one is hyper-rural. For us, it's also this idea of coming into a context and simply responding to what we see.

**Joshua Bolchover (JB):** I think the point of context is also full of contradictions. You don't go into these places and find beautiful, vernacular houses. That doesn't exist. It is a kind of ugly territory; it involves the misuse of materials, hybrids with buildings which are part vernacular, partly adapted. It's a disrupted context. There's something about the approach to find a combination between forms that are alien and forms that are very familiar. The notion of being strangely familiar is an interesting driver to some of the work that we're doing.

**Débora Mesa Molina (DMM):** The question of defining context is incredibly difficult because just interpreting each unique condition is an act of creativity in itself. Even if we all tried to be very obedient and referential to the context, the response is based on our backgrounds and knowledge. It would be completely different per person. In preparing this lecture, we realized that a lot of threads run between projects that are responding to very different questions of context. There is part of us in each project, part of who we are and how we practice. There's generally a lot of science and technicality that comes from our engineering background, and the fact that we pay a lot of attention of how things come together. But there's also aesthetics that reflect our way of creating an architecture that we don't want people to be indifferent to, because we think that architecture has a lot of power to provoke and to engage.

**DE:** It's very trendy to be vernacular; localism is "in." We've all heard in architecture school at some point that there's an appropriate response to context—geopolitically, formally, aesthetically. But at the root of vernacularism and localism, I hear a deep moralism that is frightening to consider in the twenty-first century given our discipline's history. The altruism of regional modernity suggested that there was an appropriate way to attack the site; which in my opinion was a dangerous myth to espouse largely because sites and contexts are not one thing and we typically are not hired to reinstate a site in its original form. That is the work of a conservationist. I hope that in today's world, we wouldn't be so ignorant so as to repeat that again; it led to some questionable, if not outright nefarious results. Your firms are great examples of how we can move forward without hitting the same stumbling blocks. Débora, as you said, it's about engaging the subject in new ways and evoking a different way that they might interact with a landscape, or the core of a tower, or a ger.

**DMM:** In the Montana project, if we had focused on vernacular architecture, we would have done log cabins, or we would have built a barn. For us, that was not the most powerful thing of this site, because the landscape was even more overwhelming. That was an evident point of departure.

**AGA:** I think there are two kinds of vernacularism. One is the intellectual position. The other is a coded vernacularism. For example, in Santiago de Compostela, we did two buildings in stone as required by code. You have to build in granite, but then you figure out how to crack the code. And by the way, God bless the constraints in architecture sometimes, because they are so inspiring. When you give an architect a limit, the action of breaking it becomes the driver of the project. For example, in Santiago de Compostela we wanted to be so contemporary and do things the wrong way intentionally, leaving stones rough. And then a guy from the quarry told us, "That's the way we used to do it, *a la rustica*." When they had no proper tools, they opened the stones in a similar way. So ultimately, sometimes

you arrive at an idea of process by jumping past constraints, by being aggressively contemporary, but you can also find yourself using a very tradition method that was either abandoned or reinterpreted.

**JL:** It reminds me of something that I heard Ric Scofidio say, "If you're going to be perverse, either you have to be really perverse or not at all." I'm from Taiwan, and they say, if there's a rule, then you can break it. Maybe you could say the result might be vernacular, but the approach, the method towards it, is actually radically different. That's why "appropriateness" is problematic, like the idea that there's a proper way to dress. I think we are kind of rejecting that in a sense. The ger is an interesting case, because it's for nomadic living. And ironically, it is also why the urbanization process in Ulaanbaatar has been faster than anywhere else. It's so easy to do with these structures—the most nomadic structure has accelerated an extreme urbanization. Our site is full of conflict, and there is no such thing as appropriateness. There's often a crisis of authenticity, I would say, in our sites.

**DE:** Both of your firms represent unique and contemporary models of practice that hybridize teaching and practice, nonprofit and private work. I think that the model of going out and doing architecture as a private practitioner, and getting into subjects and a range of work that isn't so profit-driven streamlines what you're doing. For those of us who love learning about building and using that as a creative driver to theorize and talk about the work, the building itself is not as important as the perspective that you get through teaching and debating that with your colleagues and through engaging other audiences. It's a circular process and requires multiple modalities of developing and executing the work including funding it yourself. This model of "multivalent" practice is incredibly rich. And the models your firms represent, students will see more and more of going forward, I suspect.

**DMM:** We started a lab within our office because we wanted to test things or build things that we had no commissions for. I mean, we would have loved to have a client that would have asked for The Truffle or the Hemeroscopium House, because that way, all the money that we gained with the other projects would not have gone into that. But it was our own decision. We needed to do things. We needed to research. The domestic scale was perfect for that. It was something that we could finance and that also allowed us to then do other projects. We would have probably not done the project in Montana if our client had not seen The Truffle. Similarly, the other project that we showed—the house where we are testing these very lightweight construction systems—has allowed us to prove that there are other ways of building housing, and this leads to discussions with developers about how to translate that into collective housing. This is also our way to escape getting pigeon holed, where people expect you to always do the same thing.

Débora Mesa Molina, Antón García-Abril, David Erdman, John Lin, and Joshua Bolchover (in order from left to right) in conversation at Pratt Sessions 04

Steven
Holl

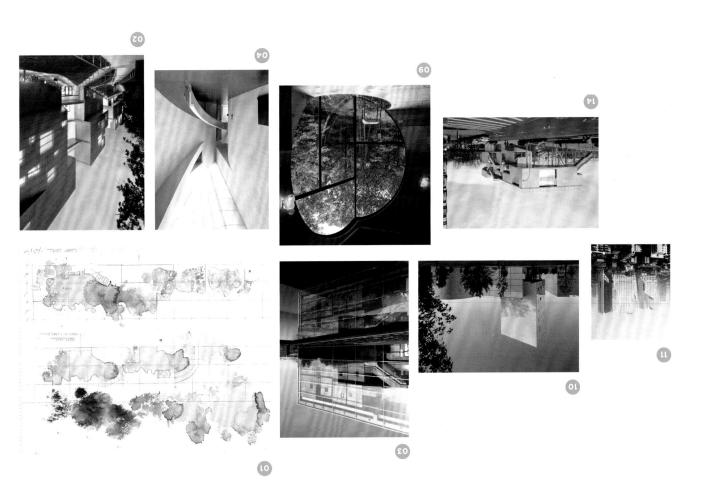

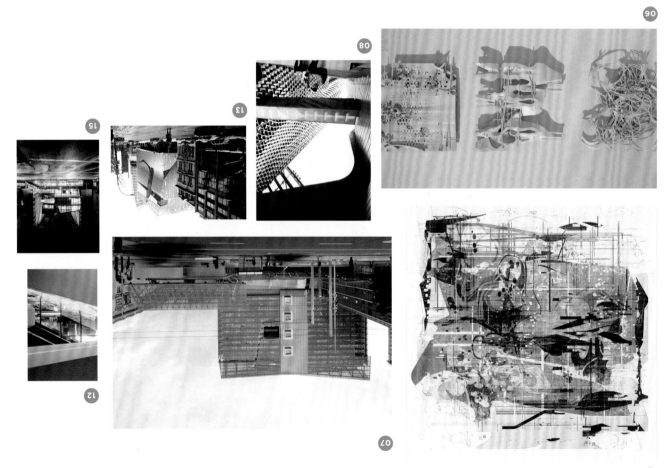

# Introduction

**DAVID ERDMAN**

Tonight's speakers, Thom Mayne and Steven Holl, have engaged a breadth of context and scales few architects have had a chance to. They have written about, reflected upon, and speculated about their work at a range of scales, and they have a willingness to **understand context** as something which is **discursive**. Something that has to do with **method**, as much as with the **physics of the site**.

Something evident in both their many works is the presence of the hand; which gives the work a human impact. The idea of the "handmade" is somewhat of an impossibility for the architect, as we don't *make* architecture ourselves. And that's certainly not the way that either of these architects attack it. It is, however, a productive way to understand how we engage context, or give buildings a sense of authenticity that's not tied to place. Let's call it an **intentional imperfection** as a starting point; a characteristic the HBO dramatic television series *Westworld* uses to encapsulate "free will" and what distinguishes humans from artificial intelligence.

Take, for example, Steven's delicate watercolors. 01 Many of these describe circuitry or massing; giving the machinic, logistic or geometric a "sketchiness" and fluidity. The medium of watercolor is also conceptualized and deployed in his buildings and as a means of **engaging their surroundings**.

The *bleed* that one can create with watercolor painting isn't doable in oil, you can't do it in acrylic, with pen, or graphite. Water leaks into the grain of the paper, which in Steven's work is **literalized as a contextual effect**, producing a dynamic interplay between interior and exterior. There's also a blotchy quality to some of Steven's buildings that gives them a depth and a relation to their surroundings. 02 This imperfection too could be understood as being born out of the dynamic pooling and saturation densities of watercolor. The projects are often on or around water and combined with reflective water bodies 03 where these qualities can be magnified, further confounding where the boundary of the building is. Finally and perhaps the most sensate of these is a distinct **capillary action** in his buildings. 04 The way that water is pulled into the paper, one might be able to talk about how the cracks and fissures in some of his work **pull light into the voids and masses** or pulls humans vertically through the building mass.

Thom's models and drawings have a very different set of qualities by comparison. In his early models, a mixture of Bondo and acrylic paint gives massing a **vivid sense of buildup**, 05 or accumulation. It extends into the drawings, where you see a thickness and depth. And in more recent "drawings," (actually 3D printed models combining drawing and modeling called "paintings") there is a scratchiness, almost like an etching, or carving. The implied action of the hand or a tool, rake, etch induces the sense of an **eroded palimpsest** 06 in his drawings and models; striking when one understands they are entirely digital.

These are devices that we also see in the buildings of Morphosis. There are mixed panel types that produce predominantly matte finish, resonating with those buildings' muted contextual effects. This finishing technique seen as an analogue for an operational strategy could be construed as a contextual "patina." Thom's buildings have a patinated quality visually and a visceral sense of the hand, but they also "sneak" into their surroundings in a subtle way. The double skin screens so predominant in many projects are absorbent. 07 There's an intense layering of line work that's delicate and light from afar, but it gets richer, and more vivid, as we move deeper into the projects. In more recent work, there's bas-relief. The **grooving** (or more recently an apparent **plucking)** forms an **immersive spatial and textural preamble,** 08 that either wraps the exterior or leaks out and pulls one into the project.

The work of both Steven and Thom has a highly-sophisticated organizational formalism, **which embraces methods of both addition and subtraction**. This combination of moves is not a device to be underestimated or overlooked. The dexterity and capacity of those forms to graft into the context physically and socio-politically is an evident byproduct of their willingness to composite these kinds of techniques; it gives them a sense of being incomplete or open and porous.

Yet they seem to come at this from opposite starting points. Steven's figural subtraction—slicing and booleaning—is extremely compelling and evident in a number of his projects. 09 There are moments and scales where this is composited with additive methods. 10 11 Thom's work has a layering and additive sensibility. He works with **accumulation**, but it's rarely, if ever, singular. There are always subtractive elements in there 12 —cracking, concavity, and slicing—that activate the negative space in the tissue of the project, connecting it to its surroundings. 13

Though Steven and Thom are among few architects pushing the limits of density and exploring the degree to which high density is inhabitable. They are both building and **designing for densities** that aren't yet familiar to mainstream community development. Both explore an **artificially infused compactedness**, where circuitry seems to hemorrhage out of buildings or connects to otherwise separate buildings. (14) Some buildings serve as prototypes for future contexts and scales of density, and among each of them harbor an indisputable sense of urban interiority; (15) moving across scales and resulting in large scale involutions of light and texture that permeate, dilate, and expand the interiors of otherwise compact, dense mass.

Finally, key is an ability to expand their practices to engage architecture and landscape, a component of any twenty-first century densified city. Landscape is no longer that which is left over, or relegated solely to a roof or a wall, but is **constructed, folded, and enmeshed into their buildings**. While their moved may start from different origins, they are certainly shared practices between them and through which they engage context. Ranging from notions of the humane to the engagement with constructed grounds we can understand the close relationship of medium and context; the two subjects of the Pratt Sessions. Through Thom and Steven's work we might begin to understand or speculate on how context could be theorized as a medium to be worked with, altered, and reshaped; aggressively and in ways that tie architecture to both existing and future environments. Through this framework, I am certain an entertaining and insightful discussion will emerge in this historic gathering of the minds.

# Steven Holl

## NEW YORK, NY

It's a pleasure to be here and to see so many friends. I went back into my files to find the first picture ever taken of Thom and me, when we met thirty-three years ago. I knew his work and he knew my work, even though we were both just starting out. But we were both obsessive. It's an honor to be able to be together tonight, and be obsessive about whatever this word "context" means.

When I wrote my first manifesto, I was dealing with the word *context*. It was called "Anchoring." It was 1988, the height of post-modernism. Contextualism was the word, and for most people, context meant that you had to make buildings that looked like everything around it. Others said that the real context is the time we live in; that architecture should be about our time. Someone wrote about my work that the context was phenomenology, that there was a shift from deconstruction and language-based theory to phenomenology—experientially-based theory.

Context is still important in my work today. Right now, we're working on a small community library in Queens, on

Steven Holl Architects, Hunters Point Community Library, Queens, NY, 2018

the waterfront across from Louis Kahn's Four Freedoms Park memorial. The library is right in front of a series of glass developer towers in Hunters Point. One of the developers proposed to put the library in three or four stories at the bottom of a tower, if they could build it on our site. But the council man Jimmy Van Bremer said, "No, this has to be a public building with a public presence." We designed the library to be vertical instead of horizontal. There was enough room to make it all horizontal, but I wanted the library to have a view over the skyline, to give the view back to this community library.

As you move up through the section of the building, you browse through the books, but behind the books are computer desks. The whole library is about the digital and the book. There's a community hall, a children's section, an adult section, and a teen section. And this is all public space with a viewing deck at the top.

Another current project is in Richmond, Virginia. When we were invited to do an institute for contemporary art at Virginia Commonwealth University, I started to study the old site. We found that there used to be railroad tracks on the site. Today, this site is a bridge between the university's campus and downtown Richmond. This Institute for Contemporary Art is going to be a place where the students can have their end of the year shows, and where outside exhibitions will be shown. It will be about art today and tomorrow.

In thinking about art, we realized it no longer has a grand narrative. In the twentieth century, for example, we had a Cubist period, then an Abstract Expressionist period in the 1950s, but we find ourselves today without a grand narrative. We thought about this as "Forking Time," a term used by Jorge Luis Borges. For us it presented the notion that today different narratives that can exist as parallels in time. Brice Marsden can continue to paint and Doug Aitken can continue his video work.

In our design, these parallel narratives branch out as three gallery spaces from what I call the "plane of the present," which looms up to create a fourth gallery, which is the undefined gallery. In this sense, its context is really about time.

Another part of its context is, of course, location. It's Richmond, Virginia—a place where you're told that you have to build in brick. The building has a very complicated concept, but I was surprised that when we presented it to the board that was hiring us and to some people from the university, they loved the idea, and it was on the front page of the *Richmond Times*. I think that is because the building is about art and students, which should be about the future. All good reasons why a non-brick building should be built in Richmond.

We just completed an academic building in Iowa, where we were our own context. This new building is adjacent to

Steven Holl Architects, Institute for Contemporary Art, Virginia Commonwealth University, Richmond, VA, 2018

a building we did in 2007. The older building is made out of corten steel, and it's planar and horizontal. At the beginning of the design phase for the new building, I had a crisis, because I thought, "It's a campus. Should this new building also be corten, so it would be like a context of a campus?" I struggled with this for a while. I had thirty designs that were corten steel. Until I decided, "No, it shouldn't be corten. In fact, it should be a different material and idea altogether." So, unlike the older building, the new building is vertical, volumetric, and all concrete. The simple idea is that this laminar section shifts and creates courts of light in the building.

In Houston, we're working on the Museum of Fine Arts, which lies at the corner of two main streets. In the competition brief, the rule was that you had to build a seven-story parking garage, in order to free up a main parking lot where the new gallery pavilion would be built. The MFAH campus is made up of a Mies Van Der Rohe building from 1958 and 1978, an original stone building from 1924, and a Rafael Moneo building from 2000. The campus also has one of Noguchi's greatest sculpture gardens.

In the competition, we broke the rules. Rather than building a new parking garage, we proposed building a new Glassell School of Art, and to put the parking underneath and connect everything below ground. We knew that it was a risk because if they picked us, they would have to build an extra building. But they did!

Steven Holl Architects, Visual Arts Building, University of Iowa, Iowa City, IA, 2016

Steven Holl Architects, Visual Arts Building, University of Iowa, Iowa City, IA, 2016

Steven Holl Architects, Lewis Arts Complex, Princeton University,
Princeton, NJ, 2017

Steven Holl Architects, Hunters Point Community Library, Queens, NY, 2018

Steven Holl Architects, Ex of IN House, Rhinebeck, NY, 2016

Steven Holl and Thom Mayne

# Thom Mayne

## LOS ANGELES, CA

In the fifteen minutes that I have to make an opening presentation tonight, I want to show a few projects; a morphology of public space. Today, especially in the United States, I think we are continually organizing and developing an idea of context.

Caltrans District 7 Headquarters was a building that we won in a competition. In Los Angeles public space is not a given at all. But we won the competition because we produced the public space that was anticipating a potential of a public that has no interest in that. We produced a space that activated itself. We understood it as a limited set of opportunities, and we activated it with various notions that were very particular to Los Angeles.

Another one, that's a little more particular, is our project in Paris—Phare Tower. There were opportunities to focus on the reconfiguration and re-origination of public space. When we started this competition, it was clear that it was all about connection. The site is the end of the number one line and the

Morphosis, Caltrans District 7 Headquarters, Los Angeles, CA, 2005

end of the Champs-Élysées. It was important to think about the re-connection of movement to a station that accommodates 500,000 people a day. In addition, it was an opportunity to rethink the very generic building type of the office tower. This is an idiosyncratic project. You have to approach it through the project's highly specific characteristics, which could be seen as problematic—the lack of site, for example. We developed a building that was complex, in terms of its public stature, focusing on the public nature of this site as it connected to the main transportation network.

In Cincinnati, this connection activity is operating at an urban scale. And when we were selected to design the Campus Recreation Center, the University of Cincinnati had been bringing in architects to do "icon buildings." They were using it as a way of increasing the presence of the campus. By the time they got to us, they started realizing the limitations of the singularity of icons and they were instead getting interested in connectivity. The whole focus of our project had to do with a broad, urban connection of a campus. The building was a non-object, centered around connectedness and transparency. We strove for diversity of spaces that promoted interconnection between academic housing, recreational areas, service spaces, et cetera.

We wanted to find the level of complexity that we see in the built historic city. That includes accident and chance. As you move through this building, it continually reinvents itself, as some sort of a broad, connective tissue which continues from exterior to interior.

The focus of our building at 41 Cooper Square was public activity. This could be the departure point of a more or less generic building; with labs, classrooms, and faculty offices. But it became the focus of the broader educational and social pedagogy of Cooper Union, which was claiming to connect engineers, artists, and architects. And the notion was, in fact, to break down the difference between those disciplines, so that the project was focused on a singular, eleven-story vertical piazza. We used skip-stop elevators to produce a social density and transparency, and promote connectivity and dialogue. In addition, it was connecting Cooper Union to the city, as a part of the intellectual creative capital that makes the density of New York.

Using some of these ideas in a single building, but heading in a different direction, is our Emerson College building—a Los Angeles outpost for a Boston school, and I was fascinated with the discrepancy between Boston and LA. I would say that they are two extremes of cities, culturally. I was involved in choosing a site, and we selected a site on Sunset Boulevard with a perfect view of the Hollywood sign. The building was very

Morphosis, University of Cincinnati Campus Recreation Center, Cincinnati, OH, 2005

much about making this large interior space. The housing is on the perimeter, while the academic and administrative spaces are in the middle. Similar to the building at Cooper Union, the stair and its approach to a public park, on the fifth level, is about a social conduit. In this case, we got fascinated with the notion of a density and congestion. We looked for moments of compression and opportunities to occupy the spaces between, which could be seen as quasi-accidental.

The construction of site is typical in cities like Los Angeles, Dallas, and Houston. Typically, sites in these cities have no qualities in an urban sense, and certainly within a broader public sense. For the Perot Museum in Dallas we were interested not only in constructing a site, but a site that was starting to move towards landscape. This is a natural history museum, so the relationship of landscape to building became primary.

This building is not really in the city. It is across from a freeway, and in many ways, it's not a correct site for a public building. We were interested in making clear that the user of this building is still part of public life in the city. As visitors move up through the building, the escalator is moving out, so you're moving away from the building and into the city. When you get to the top, as you're entering the first exhibit space, you're in the city in psychological terms. We wanted to challenge the suburban framework of a city like Dallas.

Morphosis, 41 Cooper Square, New York, NY, 2009

Morphosis, Phare Tower, Paris, France, 2006-2010

Morphosis, 41 Cooper Square, New York, NY, 2009

Steven Holl and Thom Mayne

Morphosis, Perot Museum of Nature and Science, Dallas, TX, 2012

Morphosis, Emerson College Los Angeles, Los Angeles, CA, 2014

Steven Holl and Thom Mayne

# Conversation

## STEVEN HOLL AND THOM MAYNE

**Steven Holl (SH):** David, one of the most interesting things to see was the image of all these books about context that you showed in your introduction. Each of them was a manifesto. What I find lacking today is that critical dialogue. I remember reading *Collage City* (1978), and thinking that this was only presenting a planometric argument, even though a city is sectional. I also remember *Learning From Las Vegas* (1972), which I hated completely. Kevin Lynch's *Image of the City* (1960) was what I was looking at when I went to school, and somehow, it's valid again. In the same way, Steen Eiler Rasmussen's *Experiencing Architecture* (1962) is valid again. It's almost like the theories go around and come back again. We just went off the track for a moment.

**Thom Mayne (TM):** Someone told me yesterday that 30 percent of all architecture has been built in the last thirty or fifty years. We invent context, we're not operating within the found city. But it's also not any longer ideological in those terms. We have options. I can produce a conventional space, which is appropriate for a particular project, or I can invent something that's much more unique to an invention of something. Ideology closes you down in a way that's just not interesting. You need malleability today. I looked at this selection of books on context and thought, "oh my God, we still look at this stuff? This is ridiculous."

**SH:** It's not ridiculous, because those were very thoughtful works.

**TM:** We no longer need that as a guideline.

**SH:** What we're missing is the dialogue. We don't have anything that we can put up on the screen and say this is representative of our conversation today.

**TM:** See, you're an east coast guy, I'm a west coast guy. You need books to look at. Can't the theory come out of the work as another option, versus the work coming out of the theory?

**SH:** But if you don't have the theory in your own mind, someone else has to read it into your work.

**TM:** That's not my problem. I'm not a theorist, I'm an architect.

**SH:** You wouldn't negate someone who had quite a lot of knowledge, reading into your work, a possible way to read it.

**TM:** If it's useful, of course.

**SH:** Tonight, for the first time, you and I were compared. There are a number of things we connect on, like the tactile, the haptic realm, the detail, and the material. When I first came to SCI-Arc—I think you invited me to lecture there in 1985—I went to 72 Market Street, and the obsession of the details was so inspiring to me. Carlo Scarpa's Querini Stampalia foundation in Venice is still there, and that little garden has more power in the details, in the space, in the feeling of the geometry, the light, the water, than there is in half of the work that today's 200-person firms do.

**TM:** We've been friends for thirty years, and I would have said, in terms of strategy, we're exactly opposite. We couldn't be further apart.

**SH:** I would agree with that.

**TM:** You sit down, you make a watercolor, and you have a total, singular understanding...

**SH:** It's called an idea that drives the design.

**TM:** That's right—an idea that drives the design. I work collectively and through dialogue. I'm interested in something that comes out of a strategy that allows me to produce something that's beyond my ability to cognitively understand that thing and it goes beyond my ability to organize something. I believe in the operational strategy, and I'm totally disinterested in any kind of meaning of where it first comes from. I'm interested in evaluating that strategy for a certain set of performances and conceptual evaluations. That becomes the beginning of a conversation that takes us to different places. For students, that would represent a very different notion of self and of your relationship to defining a project. When you look at our project at Cooper Union, there was no a priori idea. Instead the discussion was about how architecture participates, and the focus had to be with the connectivity between these three disciplines. The project started with a space and with that came the density of the site, which now starts concretizing an idea within spatial terms. So, it came from the beginning of an idea that wasn't about architecture as a formal idea. In fact, it's kind of an odd-looking building. I'm actually kind of ambivalent towards it. I'm going to probably prefer the conceptual path over my subjective notion of beauty.

**SH:** You just argued for the total, empirical start, without a conceptual a priori idea. I have to find an a priori idea that drives the design. It brings together all the manifold pieces—a complex program, a client who is running all over, the budget. In the Visual Arts Building in Iowa the ideas of the laminar shift and five centers of light work together to have an identity that's very different from the adjacent planar, horizontal building. I can show you maybe fifty designs before landing at this one. I had a real crisis with that project, because I couldn't find the idea that was going to drive it, that I could communicate to my staff and to the client. But once I found the idea that drove the design,

we could do the building. I think your early work was closer to my work, in the sense that there was an idea. The 2-4-6-8 House had a very clear idea.

**TM:** That was typological nonsense.

**SH:** There were these ten things that occupied the space. That was an idea that's driving a design.

**TM:** We were connected in materiality and our interest in micro/macro. When walking into Higgins Hall at Pratt, you are directly connected to the building by touching the custom designed door handle. We shared that interest in craft. But I'm moving towards an urban scale in projects, and I'm looking for the urban type of complexity. To get back to the conversation on context: it seems to me that projects today have to do with ever-increasing organizational complexities, that have to be done in a quicker and quicker time. Steven, you often say that architecture takes eight to ten years to do. We're trying to do it in eight months. That's where the world's going, and there's no reason that it can't be done. It's not our choice, as architects, by the way. We have to behave in a different way, if we're going to operate in a contemporary world.

**David Erdman (DE):** I think you both come from very different directions, but what I find astonishing is that the qualities of your representational techniques—some made by hand, other appearing like they were made by hand—end up in both of your buildings; as different as your hands may be. There's a discussion in the discipline about authenticity, which relies on connecting the work closely to a place. I think

your work, collectively, is evidence that this is not a given. There's a way to work in a number of places; giving projects a certain discursive context and set of qualities that are open-ended enough to produce some sense of value and humane attachment to the architecture, its rituals and practices; which I suppose we could call authenticity.

**SH:** Certainly, the technology has a big role to play. We're both using state of the art model making techniques. But I start with my hand and my mind at 6:00am with a 5 by 7-inch watercolor, then I bring it in to the office, the team draws it up into a 3D model, they put it into the CNC or they print it overnight. The whole process continues digitally.

**DE:** Can you intentionally re-originate a site? Can you give it a new origin?

**TM:** Yeah, absolutely. Today, operating at this larger urban scale, with the tools we have, and the relationship to infrastructure, this is becoming increasingly central to our work. We can absolutely transform a site. It's more than that; you can construct site. The site becomes project, and it's no longer passive site versus active building. I think that will be one of the paradigm shifts that takes place. And in fact, I would claim that the operation of the site might be, in many cases, the most interesting part of a project. And in the case of the Perot Museum in Dallas, the piece on top was more or less generic, and the site was the project.

David Erdman (left), Thom Mayne (center), and Steven Holl (right) in conversation at Pratt Sessions 06

Introduction

# Overview

# Dean's Note

## TOM HANRAHAN
## DEAN OF THE SCHOOL OF ARCHITECTURE

*Pratt Sessions* is a new publication developed by the Graduate Architecture and Urban Design programs in Pratt Institute's School of Architecture. The school has long been host to a series of innovative publications that not only introduced readers to emerging ideas in architecture and design but presented them in new and experimental forms. Over three decades the *Pratt Journal, In Process* and *TARP* have expanded the boundaries of theoretical, visual, and topical design journals. *Pratt Sessions* joins this distinctive group with its own inventive format, and rich array of completed work and theoretical speculations by some of the most important architects and designers practicing today.

Each section of *Pratt Sessions* is a transcribed public conversation between paired designers and architects, augmented by examples of their work and observations and questions by moderator and chair of Graduate Architecture and Urban Design David Erdman. The results are provocative and unexpected and provide insights into architecture and design that are not always revealed in more traditional lecture formats. Some of these conversations demonstrate broad agreement on critical ideas in design, while others illustrate the unique differences in approach and thinking from this exceptionally talented group of contributors. All of them touch on the most important issues affecting the design of spaces, buildings, and cities today. Together they illustrate the remarkable range and complexity of thought that can be found in today's design world.

The participants in the sessions are curated as much for their similarities as they often are for their differences. They are asked to focus short presentations on the given subject as a means of enriching a precise discourse and (perhaps most importantly) to foster student discussion; a central factor in the origins of the series. The discussions have extended for hours after presentations completed and are all followed by continued debate and discussion during the reception and Pop-Up Exhibition, including work from two artists the participants have nominated. The artist inclusions often further enriched the discourse and potential affiliations with subjects and other discourse networks—bearing the fruits of being housed within an art, architecture, and design institute such as Pratt.

My job as the introducer of these events has been not so much to laud my esteemed colleagues (which would be easy and perhaps in line with the traditional introduction) nor account for their work in a manner accurate to either their writing or others' writings about their work. Instead it has been to give their work a narrow reading in relation to the theme at hand. I see my introductions, included here with the presentations and conversations, as one part warm up band—priming the arena for the main act—and one part having a productively oblique relationship to what the presenters may or may not show; which was often not known in advance.

This first volume of Pratt Sessions collects six sessions, three focused on each subject, involving fourteen participants, spanning one year. While each section is presented chronologically within the two subjects, they are not in the exact order in which they occurred over the course of the year. The subjects and lectures were "interdigitated," allowing for a switching from one subject to the other to unfold over the semester and year. This produced a rich texture of thinking, a range of opinions, and a productively selective amnesia about the subjects at hand. A distinct advantage to distributing a symposium and/or discussion with this type of structure is its redundancies and bifurcations.

The book design is multi-axial in response, using different page orientations—front, back, portrait, and landscape—to coalesce. This was the graphic counterpart to infusing the book with productive yet coarse mixtures of readings with the hope that one might flip between all three sections, and discover this introduction, for example, well after reading other portions of the book. The middle section of this volume collects the proper "front" of the book; now dislocated to the center and in a different page orientation. It gathers introductory material, including the essay by Catherine Ingraham, introduction by Tom Hanrahan, and the Pop-Up Exhibition artists and artworks. The two sessions sections are mirrored, forming a palindromic structure that allows for reading in two directions. They include the introductions I delivered as well as the edited versions of the participants' presentations and the conversations that followed. The book is designed to enable the reader to experience and navigate multiple sessions, browsing and "surfing" between subjects, introductions, and presentations.

This first collection owes a great deal to its participants who willingly dove into somewhat unpredictable territory. It is my opinion that it is within this zone of the session that we are the most aware and engaged. It is when those flows switch and reverse, open up counterintuitive readings and understandings that one might find a trajectory through the discourse valuable to his or her own work, thinking, or studies.

# Introduction

**DAVID ERDMAN
CHAIRPERSON, ASSOCIATE PROFESSOR
GRADUATE ARCHITECTURE + URBAN DESIGN**

In surfing, a "session" is a period in which you make something out of nothing. A moment of precision, in which one reads, galvanizes, exploits, and interacts with a consortium of forces. It is as euphoric as it is fleeting, as mysterious as it is understood. Surfers spend their lives craving a good session.

The musical equivalent is not so different. Often unpaid, informal gatherings harnessing live performance or improvised recording, one could argue that a good musical session (if witnessed or documented) is the engine behind a musician's growth. Be it musician to musician, human to aquatic medium or architect to architect, the spirit of the Pratt Sessions is to debate, question and discuss matters on the periphery and core of our discipline. To capture a fleeting moment with some precision and allow it to alter, shift, and transform dynamically.

Dean Tom Hanrahan and I have conceived the Pratt Sessions as a distributed symposium focused on two parallel research subjects we are currently examining at in the Graduate Architecture and Urban Design programs; Architectural Mediums and Architectural Contexts. Like a surfing session, these sessions are meant to galvanize something out of subtle aberrations, to read the surface closely, to gain an understanding of its depths, and to have an improvisational one-off quality; each discussion being different and having to negotiate the particularities of that specific event and its participants.

Bringing together pairings of designers and thinkers, one of whom is regional and the other non-regional (predominately from New York City and Los Angeles), the sessions curb stereotypes and assumptions about the thermohaline circulation of architecture discourse; I am here borrowing heavily from surfology, using the term for oceanic swells and current flows as an analogy for the formation of the Kittler–like

discourse networks in architecture. Thermohaline circulation, or THC as it is otherwise known, has the added benefit of further deepening an allusion to the euphoria associated with titillating and redistributing those networks, which is important to the Pratt Sessions.

The circuitry of architecture discourse has been in an East to Westward flow in North America, since its instantiation in the late nineteenth and early twentieth century, and reinscribed and stabilized through the mid- and late twentieth century. One could chart this as Ivy to Prairie to the Wild Wild West. The intellectual culture of architecture with its flows and establishments thus re-inscribe Manifest Destiny often with a pejorative set of associated overtones: the East is where you think about it and the West is where you just do it! Laid back versus uptight, sunny versus cloudy, the climatological and cultural overtones continued to segregate and divide East and West Coast cultures and discourse networks until the late twentieth century when they began to reverse.

The mechanics of these established modalities of thinking, intellectual culture, and lifestyle are shifting. We feel this acutely here at Pratt – located in a primary cultural hub in Brooklyn. Back flows, ebbs, and reversals of discourse and influence can be seen across the East Coast, even seeping back into Europe where West is now influencing East. Just look at how many teachers, deans, and chairs on the East Coast are former West Coast faculty and vice versa. The curatorial approach of the sessions was to both recognize the established and historical circuitry of discourse while trying to entangle and identify its reversals and ambiguities. The sessions became an immediate and swift way to gauge the degree to which those stereotypes reassert themselves and measure where they fall apart; using the subjects of mediums and contexts as an instigator to fuel the fire.

he writes.[1] In other ways, intensification of our long-standing architectural interest in objects is, once again, leading us into object ontologies that are periously close to fetishizing what we design and produce: doors, windows, hallways, ramps, stairs, infrastructures, aesthetic shapes and forms, organizations, landscapes.

Significant ground was laid for these discussions by Robin Evans, in his 1978 essay "Figures, Doors and Passages,"[2] and, in 1996, Beatriz Colomina's book, *Privacy and Publicity*, which articulated how modernist architecture—specifically Le Corbusier and Adolf Loos—captured cinematic and photographic techniques in spaces and windows that ushered architecture into its future role as a celebrity publicist of private life. Colomina points to the strip windows of Le Corbusier's Villa Savoye and Loos' theatrical domestic space as spectral devices that bring the occupant's gaze, and architectural spaces themselves, into recursive performative modalities.[3] Le Corbusier used the reflectivity and conductivity of glass and space to mediate perception in the Villa Savoye. Computationally articulated walls in contemporary structures—such as the Broad Museum in Los Angeles—now register multiple forms of interaction between outside and inside. Case Study houses, with their L-shaped plans, also tracked our attention from the living room to the carport as a reflection on how interiority is created by exteriority.

Contemporary architects, many of whom came through the steep learning curve posed by digital architecture in the 1990s (which seemed to promise a release from conventional authorship through automatic iterative design processes) graduated from their training about five years ago into more hybridized mediations. This, in turn, has spawned renewed interest in certain periods of architectural history, such as the Renaissance and Surrealism, which should not be mistaken, however, for a neo-classical interest.

In certain hands, the hands of Elizabeth Diller and Ric Scofidio, for example, who designed the Broad Museum, many aspects of media and contexts as political and social apparatuses that govern our privacy and the subjectivity of our public selves have been articulated in architectural terms. Through their work, we have been led to see the ways in which architecture can reveal the latency of our cultural and sentient existence. Diller, whose participation in Pratt Sessions 09 will be included in Volume 2 of this publication series, has called architecture a medium and a device that can serve, inhibit or inform our passage through it. Unlike our current desire for architectural entertainment, Diller Scofidio + Renfro do not offer effect-laden fun houses. Another forerunner, Toyo Ito, in the Mediatheque, seems, by comparison, to argue for a strictly architectural approach to media. Media, Ito implies, can be announced on the interior or exterior walls of a building but the architectural uptake of communication, in the spirit of cybernetics, should pass through its structure—distortions or treatments of columns and windows. Ito wished to capture the multiple mediations of energy that constitute cultural spaces in order to understand a building as a thermodynamic machine.

The current distributive power of images on the internet is, of course, where we often end up in these conversations. The shifting character of the image itself—its proliferation and its facile production—is now at stake in any reflective study of media, mediums, contexts. What is the evidentiary status of an image now? Is it still constitutive of what can be seen and what can be articulated? The almost unavoidable curation of images, once placed in any kind of frame, is now capable of an infinity of manifestations and an erasure of referents. Images, as many have said, are a central form of social communication, but what kind of conversation is it? People visiting "sights" such as the Grand Canyon, stand on the edge of the sublime taking pictures of themselves. These selves are not Kantian selves insofar as these images do not stand for a transaction between nature and self. They stand as surrogates for a passive attendance at some already fully documented and known event. The Aggregate History Collective—a new generation of critical architectural scholars—are mapping, to some degree, paradigmatic shifts that culture seems to be making from representation to presentation. This is understood to be a crisis, and also a loss, of epistemic frameworks that have ordered knowledge in the context of modernity. Thus, at stake, in questions about media, mediums and contexts, is nothing less than the persuasiveness of our scientific paradigms, the existence of Nature with a large "N," nature with a small "n," the socio-political modelling of intelligence and knowledge, the meaning of history, the significance of language and seeing, the logics of capitalism, the fate of cities, the implications of ubiquitous computation, and questions of privacy and identity. An image of the environment is what the environment is. The map is the territory. All of which is of utmost importance in our disciplinary and practical relation to the richly texture worlds that are the object of our studies and the site of our interventions. Pratt Sessions creates an intensified climate for inquiry into both contemporary architectural work and critical frameworks, inherited and new.

[1] Bernhard Siegert, Tr. John Durham Peters, "Doors: On the Materiality of the Symbolic," in *Grey Room* (Cambridge: MIT Press, 2012) Volume -/Issue 47/ Spring 2012, p. 12.

[2] Robin Evans, *Translations from Drawing to Building and Other Essays* (Cambridge, MIT Press, 1997).

[3] Beatriz Colomina, *Privacy and Publicity: Modern Architecture as Mass Media* (Cambridge: MIT Press, 1996).

# Seeing and Articulating

CATHERINE INGRAHAM, PH.D.
PROFESSOR, ARCHITECTURAL HISTORY & THEORY
AUTHOR, *ARCHITECTURE AND THE BURDENS OF LINEARITY*

The word "media" has one definition whereas "medium" has at least thirteen definitions. Media refers to acts of communication. Medium is the milieu or environment or apparatus in which and through which communication takes place. A medium of growth, for example, allows for cellular communication. A psychic medium affords communication with the non-visible. Joshua Bolchover and John Lin (RUF)—who participated in Pratt Sessions 04—directed the 2017 Studio of Experiments in the Master of Architecture program in Graduate Architecture and Urban Design (GAUD) where they asked students to gather extensive experiential and quantifiable data about a landscape and then to de-territorialize this data into a recomposed panorama. The panoramic image became a medium that altered discussions about normative contexts such as the continuity of rural and urban landscapes. It also questioned the stability of our perceptions and the reliability of data. Contexts were rendered, in this project, as malleable.

The run-up to what we now call media, mediums and contexts has been happening for a long time—decades or centuries depending on how we position this subject matter. The concept of context, however, which is equivalent to framing, is usually understood in architecture in a fairly narrow sense. Architectural modernism claimed to repudiate contextualism, which stood for the immediate past, while architectural post-modernism claimed to restore contexts, which stood for classicism. Both movements were realized inside frameworks. Framing is what Foucault called the table of operation that makes it possible to both see and articulate the world in a particular way. What can be organized as a discourse is as crucial as what can be seen. Prior to the eighteenth-century in France, generally speaking, tables of operation did not allow people to see or articulate the meaning of fossilized bones that had been lying on the ground for millions of years. The Enlightenment figuratively

shed light on these fossils in such a way that a new table of operation emerged that afforded the reinvention of human beings as *homo sapiens*. Such frameworks are epistemic fields, in other words, the specific forms that knowledge takes at any given time, and architecture, no less than the sciences and humanities, is both implicated and instrumental in the creation of epistemic fields. Since I just broached the subject of our past as living beings, this might be the place to remind ourselves that from the moment humans stood upright, which liberated our hands and head from the ground (as the paleontologist Andre Leroi-Gourhan argued in his book *Gesture and Speech*), technological evolution has accompanied our biological evolution. For some time, however, we have been arguing about what this means. Bernard Stiegler, who founded the Institute de recherché et d'innovation at the Centre Georges-Pompidou, specifically mapped this evolution in his 2009, two-volume book, *Technics and Time*. Stiegler points to the increase of speed in technological evolution in relation to biological evolution and the manner in which technologies store human memory. It seems not too obvious to say here that the discipline and practice of architecture is a field of knowledge that explores—mediates, media-izes, contextualizes, and acts as a medium for—multiple relationships between human beings and technologies, generic and non-generic *modulars* notwithstanding. And this confirms not only what we already expect of architecture—its commitment to visual and tactile elaboration—but also what we don't expect, its commitment to the symbolic.

Media, mediums, and contexts concern the technics of representation that accompany architectural work: computing, measuring, drawing, diagramming, writing, scanning, filming, recording, and translating. And they also concern apparatuses: equipment, instruments, milieus, institutions, spaces. Architects routinely revisit the central paradoxes of architecture as an intellectual-material practice and a techno-artistic discipline. All sides of these dialectics are forms of mediation: material is a medium for ideas and ideas are a medium for material; technology is a medium for art and art is a medium for technology. There have been periods when architectural history and theory have demanded that one or the other side of these co-mediations be subordinated to the other. Material, empiricists have argued, is concrete and the concrete necessarily precedes ideas. Idealists, since Kant, do not deny the existence of materiality, but they argue that we can make nothing of materiality without ideas. We are currently in a period where aspects of architectural buildings are seen as cultural techniques that oscillate, in Bernhard Siegert's words, between *codes* (*Nomas*, laws) and *spaces* (*Topos*): "Thus space and codes shift against each other in a permanently historical way"

Stanley Saitowitz was born in Johannesburg, South Africa and received his Bachelor of Architecture at the University of Witwatersrand in 1974 and his Masters in Architecture at the University of California, Berkeley in 1977. He is an emeritus professor of architecture at the University of California, Berkeley. He has taught at numerous schools, including at the Elliot Noyes Professor, Harvard University GSD (1991-2), the Bruce Goff Professor, University of Norman, Oklahoma (1993), UCLA, Rice, SCI-Arc, Cornell, Syracuse, and University of Texas at Austin. He has given more than 200 public lectures in the United States and abroad.

His first house was built in 1975, and together with Stanley Saitowitz/Natoma Architects Inc., he has completed numerous buildings and projects. These have been residential, commercial, and institutional. He has designed houses, housing, master plans, offices, museums, libraries, wineries, synagogues, churches, commercial and residential interiors, memorials, urban landscapes, and promenades. Amongst many awards, the Transvaal House was declared a National Monument by the Monuments Council in South Africa in 1997, the New England Holocaust Memorial received the Henry Bacon Medal in 1998, and in 2006 he was a finalist for the Smithsonian Cooper Hewitt National Design Award given by Laura Bush at the White House. Three books have been published on the work, and articles have appeared in many magazines and newspapers. His paintings, drawings, and models have been exhibited in numerous galleries and museums.

Laurie Hawkinson is professor of architecture at Columbia GSAPP and partner at Smith-Miller + Hawkinson Architects (SMH+).

SMH+ is a New York City-based design studio in architecture, urban design, installations and exhibitions, objects, and products. Across the United States and abroad, SMH+ has designed public and private projects including museums, parks, transportation terminals, performing arts spaces, private residences, government facilities, a series of museum exhibitions and installations, as well as furniture and objects.

The studio's work derives inspiration from an ongoing investigation into contemporary culture, its history, and its complex changing relationship to society and contemporary ideas. The work process is transformative in the way it reinterprets basic programs and negotiate traditional craft with vanguard techniques. The office is a laboratory for speculation and making, for investigation and practice: two strands that are woven together in all of the projects from the initial concept to their final realization.

# Laurie Hawkinson

# Ensamble Studio

Ensamble Studio is a cross-functional team founded in 2000 and led by architects Antón García-Abril and Débora Mesa Molina. Balancing education, research, and practice, the office explores innovative approaches to architectural and urban spaces, and the technologies that build them. Among the studio's most relevant completed works are Hemeroscopium House and Reader's House in Madrid (Spain), Music Studies Center and SGAE Central Office in Santiago de Compostela (Spain), The Truffle in Costa da Morte (Spain), Telcel Theater in Mexico City, and, more recently, Cyclopean House in Brookline (USA), and Structures of Landscape for Tippet Rise Art Center in Montana (USA). Their work is extensively published in both printed and digital media and exhibited worldwide—Orleans Frac Centre Biennial (2017), Chicago Architecture Biennial (2017), Venice Architecture Biennale (2016 and 2010), GA International Exhibitions (2016-2010) in Tokyo, MoMA (2015), MAK Vienna (2015) MIT (2015), Bi-City Biennale of Urbanism/Architecture (2013) in Shenzhen, etc.—and awarded with international prizes: the 2017 Architizer A+Award, 2016 NCSEA Excellence in Structural Engineering Awards, Iakov Chernikhov Prize 2012, Rice Design Alliance Prize 2009 to emerging architects, Architectural Record Design Vanguard Prize 2005, among others. Beside their professional careers, both principals keep a very active research and academic agenda and have been invited professors and lecturers at numerous universities and architecture forums, were curators of Spainlab—Spanish Pavilion at the Venice Architecture Biennale 2012—and founded that same year the POPlab (Prototypes of Prefabrication Research Laboratory) at the Massachusetts Institute of Technology (MIT) that they continue to direct.

In 2005 the Chinese government announced its plan to urbanize half of the remaining 700 million rural citizens by 2030. At the same time, Joshua Bolchover and John Lin set up Rural Urban Framework (RUF), a research and design collaborative based at the University of Hong Kong. Conducted as a non-profit organization providing design services to charities and NGOs working in China, RUF has built or is currently engaged in over fifteen projects in various villages in China. The projects include schools, community centers, hospitals, village houses, bridges, and incremental planning strategies. As a result of this active engagement, RUF has been able to research the links between social, economic, and political processes and the physical transformation of each village.

The work has been exhibited in the Venice Biennale (2010), the MAK Vienna (2012) and the Guggenheim (2013). Publications include *Vitamin Green* (Phaidon, 2012), *Moderators of Change: Architecture That Helps* (Hatje Cantz, 2011), and *Rural Urban Framework: Transforming the Chinese Countryside* (Birkhauser, 2013); as well as international journals including *Architectural Record*, *Domus*, *Mark*, *Architectural Review*, and *A+U*.

RUF projects have received numerous international awards. The House For All Seasons, a rural house prototype, was awarded the WA Chinese Architecture Award in 2012, and was the overall winner of the *Architectural Review's* House Award in 2012. RUF has also received high commendations in the AR Emerging Architect Award for Recycled Brick School, Taiping Bridge Renovation, and the Qinmo Village School.

Joshua Bolchover and John Lin are currently assistant professors at the University of Hong Kong and have taught and lectured in numerous academic institutions including the Chinese University of Hong Kong; The Bartlett, UCL, Cambridge University, and the Royal Danish Academy of Fine Arts.

# Rural Urban Framework

# Steven Holl

Steven Holl was born in 1947 in Bremerton, Washington. He graduated from the University of Washington and pursued architecture studies in Rome in 1970. n 1976, he attended the Architectural Association in London, and in 1977 he established STEVEN HOLL ARCHITECTS in New York City. Considered one of America's most important architects, Steven Holl is recognized for his ability to blend space and light with great contextual sensitivity and to utilize the unique qualities of each project to create a concept-driven design. He specializes in seamlessly integrating new projects into contexts with particular cultural and historic importance. Steven Holl has been recognized with architecture's most prestigious awards and prizes. Recently, Steven Holl received the 2014 Praemium Imperiale, the 2012 AIA Gold Medal, the RIBA 2010 Jencks Award, and the first ever Arts Award of the BBVA Foundation Frontiers of Knowledge Awards (2009). In 2012, Steven Holl received the Alumnus Summa Laude Dignatus Award from the University of Washington, and has received honorary degrees from Seattle University and Moholy-Nagy University in Budapest. In 2003, he was named honorary fellow of the Royal Institute of British Architects (RIBA). In 2002 the Cooper Hewitt National Design Museum, part of the Smithsonian Institute, awarded him their prestigious National Design Award in Architecture. In 2001 France bestowed the Grande Médaille d'Or upon him, for Best Architect of the Academy of Architecture; and in the same year *Time* magazine declared him "America's Best Architect" for his "buildings that satisfy the spirit as well as the eye." Steven Holl is a tenured professor at Columbia University's Graduate School of Architecture and Planning. He has lectured and exhibited widely and has published numerous texts including *Anchoring* (1989), *Intertwining* (1996), *Parallax* (2000), *Idea and Phenomena* (2002), *Luminosity/Porosity* (2006), *House: Black Swan Theory* (2007), *Architecture Spoken* (2007), *Urbanisms: Working with Doubt* (2009), *Hamsun Holl Hamarøy* (2010), *Horizontal Skyscraper* (2011), *Color Light Time* (2012), *Scale* (2012), *Urban Hopes* (2013), and *Steven Holl* (2015). Steven Holl is a member of the American National Council of Architectural Registration Boards (NCARB), the American Institute of Architects, the American Association of Museums, the Honorary Whitney Circle, the Whitney Museum of American Art; and the International Honorary Committee, Vilpuri Library, of the Alvar Aalto Foundation.

Thom Mayne founded Morphosis in 1972 as a collective architectural practice engaged in cross-disciplinary research and design. As design director and thought leader of Morphosis, Mayne provides overall vision and project leadership to the firm. Mayne's distinguished honors include the Pritzker Prize (2005) and the AIA Gold Medal (2013). He was appointed to the President's Committee on the Arts and Humanities in 2009 and was honored with the American Institute of Architects Los Angeles Gold Medal in 2000. With Morphosis, Thom Mayne has been the recipient of twenty-six Progressive Architecture Awards, over 100 American Institute of Architecture Awards, and numerous other design recognitions. Under Mayne's direction, the firm has been the subject of various group and solo exhibitions throughout the world, including a large solo exhibition at the Centre Pompidou in Paris in 2006. Morphosis buildings and projects have been published extensively; the firm has been the subject of thirty-three monographs.

Throughout his career, Mayne has remained active in the academic world. In 1972, he helped to found the Southern California Institute of Architecture. Since then, he has held teaching positions at Columbia, Yale (the Eliel Saarinen Chair in 1991), the Harvard Graduate School of Design (Eliot Noyes Chair in 1998), the Berlage Institute in the Netherlands, the Bartlett School of Architecture in London, and many other institutions around the world. There has always been a symbiotic relationship between Mayne's teaching and practice, evidenced in his concurrent position as executive director of the Now Institute at UCLA, a research and design initiative focusing on applying strategic urban thinking to real world issues. He has been a tenured Professor at UCLA Architecture and Urban Design since 1993.

# Thom Mayne

Images of Pop-Up Exhibitions and receptions following Pratt Sessions.

# Pop-Up
# Exhibitions

In Fall 2017, the second semester of the Pratt Sessions series, we developed the idea to associate a Pop-Up Exhibition with each session; thanks to the suggestion of one of our younger faculty members who has taken on the role of our Special Projects Coordinator. As a graduate program, in an architecture school that is part of a larger art and design institute with vibrant departments of fine art, communications and industrial design, we thought it would be prudent to use the sessions to engage audiences in those related disciplines and praxes. Their works are reproduced and projected forming a point of interest and extended opportunity for debate and query during our post-session receptions; now fully instituted for every session. Pop-Up Exhibitions and artists for sessions that occurred prior to the commencement of this initiative were retrospectively selected and are included here.

Each participant has nominated an artist whose work they find compelling and related to both the subject at hand (Mediums or Contexts) and their individual work and/or interests. The specific works included in this book (and in the live exhibitions) may have been chosen by the participant, the artist or the editors of this book. Each artist and/or their representatives were involved in the process of selection where (to our pleasant surprise and on very short notice) all were receptive, supportive, often engaging us directly and often attending the sessions.

The curatorial trajectory of such a broad and open-ended initiative has a productive looseness that allows us to expand into and include other disciplines in the sessions. Some of the session participants incite the artists directly and they are all introduced in David Erdman's introductions. However, their work and the intentions behind its inclusion are often left for students and the audience to draw their own conclusions and make connections.

Whether this might be perceived as the antithesis of curation and/or an experiment in collective curation, it is nonetheless an impressive roster of artists and an indubitable collection of stunning

work. With a range of more or less established artists whose praxes oscillate from visual arts, industrial design, land art, culinary art, and just dead on intermedia the content on the following pages expands (beyond expectation) our understanding of "architectural" contexts and mediums into a broader field of intellectual discourse. Mediums ranging from photography, colossal textiles, dirt, thick viscous fluids, drawing, and cinema, each contribution allows us to draw upon not only the mediums sessions in a more focused manner, but also widen our understanding of each designer or thinker's understanding of the term.

Similarly, the manners by which artist document, replicate, falsify, mirror or reflect contexts, be it of a gallery, courtyard or landscape their work enriches and deepens the prospect of new ways to conceive of context. The following pages could perhaps be seen as a visual epilogue, a meditation on the palindromic bookends (Mediums and Contexts), on the center-piece introductions and essays, allowing one to interlace the ideas captured throughout the book and enticing one to project and explore them further.

Enrique Olvera, Octopus, *habanero, ink, ayocote, veracruzana sauce*

(Artist selected by Stanley Saitowitz)

Robert Irwin, *Scrim Veil—Black Rectangle—Natural light, Whitney Museum*

Christo and Jeanne-Claude, *Wrapped Coast, One Million Square Feet, Little Bay, Sydney, Australia*

1968–69

(Artist selected by Ensamble Studio)

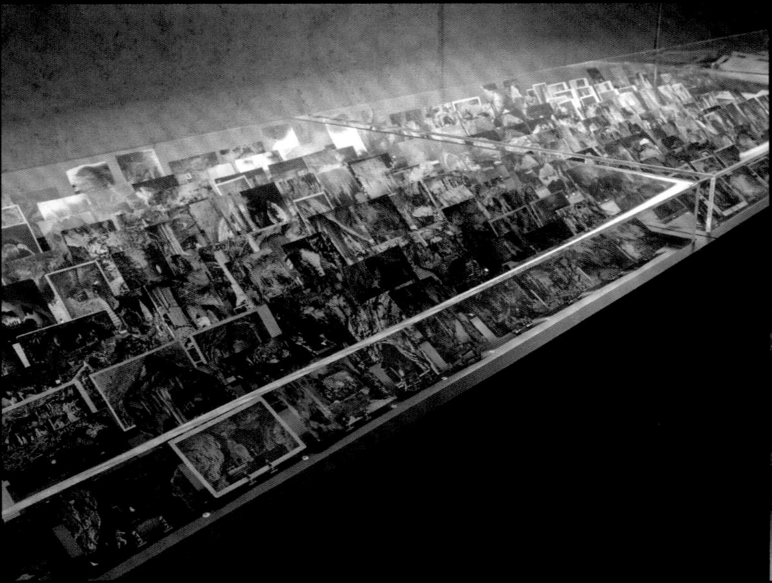

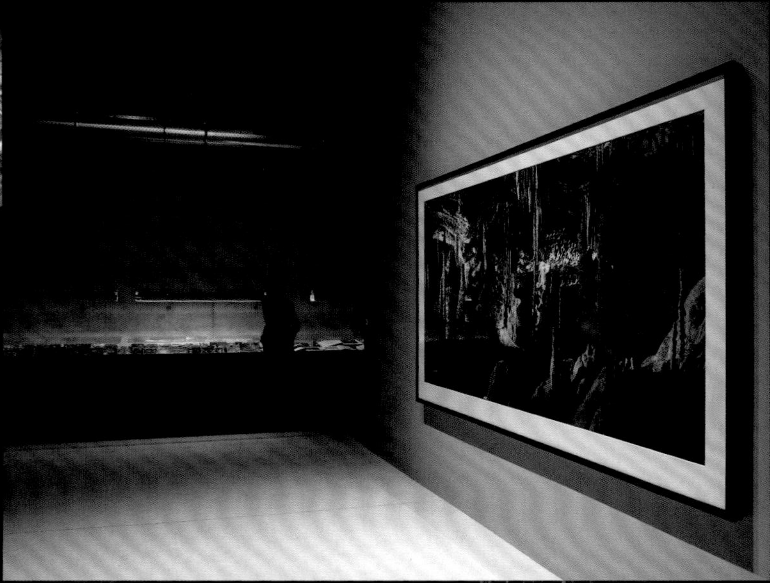

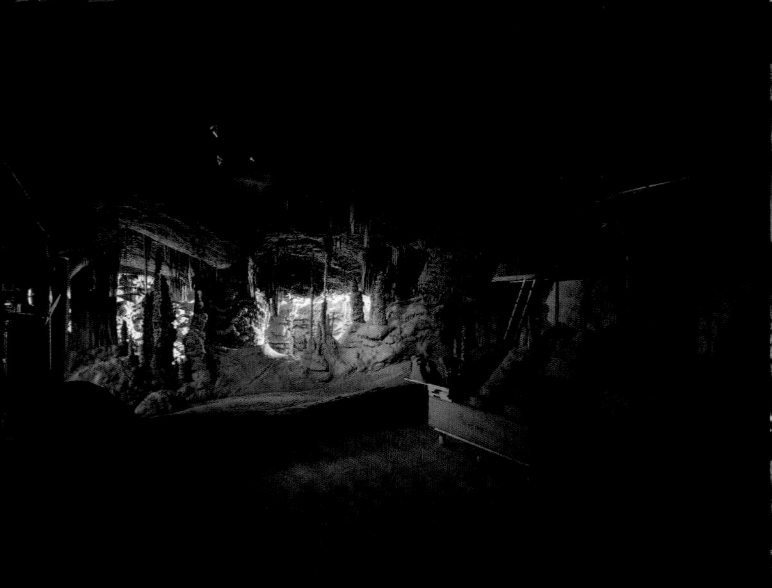

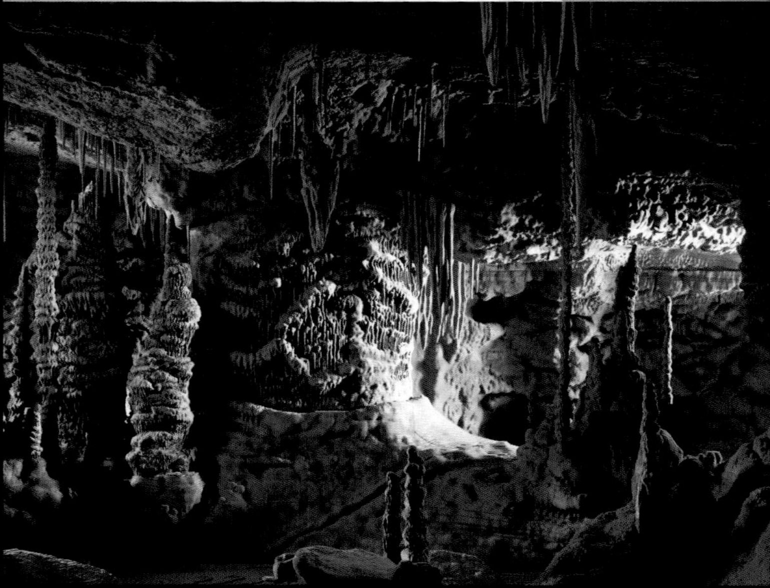

Thomas Demand, *Grotte / Grotto*
C-Print / Diasec, 198 x 440 cm, 2006